S0-BCP-668

WAYS TO COPE WITH LIFE — AND WIN!

# *Fruit from the* VINE

Also by the author

*Hope of Heaven, Joy of Earth*

**WAYS TO COPE WITH LIFE — AND WIN!**

# Fruit from the
# VINE

## An Anthology of
## Spiritual Encouragement

Compiled by
# Alice E. Flaherty

PARACLETE PRESS
Orleans, Masschusetts

*1st Printing,    September 1993*

Copyright © 1993 by Alice E. Flaherty
Library of Congress Card Number: 93-86009
All rights reserved.
Published by Paraclete Press
Orleans, Massachusetts

ISBN: 1-55725-069-3
Printed in the United States of America

*To*

*John, Carly, and Alex*

*Grandchildren Extraordinaire*

*and another one soon to be born*

# Acknowledgements

My warmest thanks to the following special people who helped make this book a reality. Each and every one of them exhibited a helpful attitude and an enthusiastic spirit:

All of the authors and pastors who so generously contributed to this, my favorite collection of encouraging messages and writings.

Paraclete's Senior Editor David Manuel and his Staff for believing in the potential of this book, and for giving me the opportunity to share it with people who are trying to cope successfully with life's problems and heartbreaks.

Don Crawford, Literary Consultant, free lance author and editor, who served as my agent. His help and counsel were invaluable.

Dave Came, a good friend and managing editor of a leading publishing house, for his encouragement and expert counsel.

John Flaherty, my husband, proofreader par excellence, who faithfully read all the pages of the manuscript, making corrections and offering constructive suggestions.

David K. Hardin, President of the Chicago Sunday Evening Club, and Executive Assistant Connie Escalante for their hearty cooperation and assistance.

Frances Liptrap, Ruth Freeman, Sue Neuschel, Susan Payne, Jinny Strong, John and Lorraine Bellingham, Jeanne Sevigny, and Ruthy Villavicencio, all knowledgeable Christian friends, who looked over different parts of the manuscript, and who served as an excellent sounding-board, always ready with their candid reactions and encouragement.

# Contents

# Preface

It has been said that every Christian should have a personal ministry. If so, then mine is the ministry of encouragement. It was not always so, but after going through several deep valleys in my life, I emerged much more aware of others who were suffering sorrow or illness. After experiencing a rebirth of faith, the Bible came alive for me, and my enthusiasm for reading inspirational books grew as well. My library is filled to overflowing. I am also a sermon-saver. Yes, a sermon-saver. I have been saving my favorites for years. The encouragement and wisdom I have gleaned from them have contributed greatly to my spiritual well-being.

So here I offer you a few of my prized "collectibles"— an assortment of inspiring messages from the outstanding Christian authors and pastors who have so generously contributed some of their wisdom and love to this book. Just as they have helped me, I trust that what they say here will strengthen your faith and lift your spirit to a new level of confidence in God's love and plan for your life.

These authors and pastors come from many different areas of the United States, as well as from different denominational backgrounds. However, as you read, you will sense their common bond of faith in God and their love for Christ. Their concern for others is obvious, as is their desire to help people cope successfully with life's little problems, as well as with the big ones like tragedy and sorrow.

Even though each chapter is complete in itself, I suggest you start with the first chapter and read each one as it comes. You will notice that the book begins with my lamenting the fact that life is so often unfair, disappointing, and sometimes downright devastating. But as you continue reading, you will see how the chapter-content progresses from problems to solutions, and finally how you can *make sure* that one day God will "wave you across" the finish line and declare you a *winner!*

Alice E. Flaherty
Park Ridge, Illinois

# Introduction

Sometimes I feel like crying out to God, "How long, O Lord? How much longer must the world continue to endure one catastrophe after another? Couldn't you just wind it up and take us all Home?"

There is so much tragedy around me, terrible accidents and illnesses that have struck family members and close friends. When I add on all the insurmountable problems the world is facing today, I can't help asking God how much more people can take, particularly those who are suffering painful and prolonged illnesses, unemployment, crime, famine, and war.

But my Christian common sense tells me to back off and let God be God. He is the one who will decide when the time is right to call His people Home. And I remind myself how He has led me safely through some frightening valleys—valleys I wouldn't want to repeat. He has sent guardian angels to rescue me from life-threatening situations, and helped me in countless other ways when I have needed His guidance and protection.

So what should we do, when life isn't fair? Ask God to stop the world and let us get off? Or shall we "hang in there" and keep trying? Personally, I would rather stay and "fight the good fight of faith!" I have lived long enough to have lost some of the battles, but I have won some, too—some glorious ones!

Jesus understands our cries of anguish, because He, too, cried out to God to deliver Him from the agony He had to endure. Nevertheless, not my will, but Thine, be done. Job cried out, and so have countless other people when confronted by horrendous circumstances. I think of my sister, confined to her bed for so many months before she died, because of severe arthritis. I think of my brother and his wife, whose oldest son, Michael, has been hospitalized in an intensive care unit for more than two years with a devastating case of encephalitis. Part of his brain has been destroyed, and he is now blind. But he understands what has happened to him and wants desperately to get well and go home. You can imagine the suffering he, his wife, and their whole family are having to endure. Family members take turns going to the hospital every day to help care for him. Add to that heart-breaking situation the fact that Michael's younger brother, Max, a captain in the Air Force, was killed in a plane crash. To lose one son would seem to be enough, wouldn't it? But two?

I have a friend whose parents once lived on a large farm in Indiana. One day they went into town to visit a friend in the hospital. While they were gone, a tornado roared across the countryside and literally blew away their house and barns—everything! Unfair? To be sure! But the other side of the coin is that by going to see their sick friend, their lives were saved.

Ironic, isn't it, how blessings are always mixed in with our trials? We cannot control what God allows to befall us—but we do have total control over how we respond to it. My brother and sister-in-law tell how thankful they are for the love and support of their two daughters, for their many loyal friends, and for the way God is helping them cope. And it is inspiring to see how Michael's wife is holding on to her faith.

How about you? Are you also currently facing one or more seemingly unfair circumstances in your life? Or maybe you're walking along on a relatively pleasant plateau right now—but how would you react if your life were suddenly invaded by a catastrophic illness, a tornado, or a terrible accident? Would you scream at God that life is not fair? You might, but after absorbing the shock, you would probably begin to pray and ask God for help and courage to carry on.

We do indeed live in a very unfair and mixed-up world. God didn't intend it to be that way. His original plan was for us to live in Eden, a perfect place. Rather than create us as robots, however, He gave us a will and the freedom to choose whether to love Him or reject Him. And as we all know, the human spirit has been vacillating between good and evil ever since.

So what should our reaction be when life confronts us with an unfair interruption? There really are only two choices: Either accept what has happened with a calm and trusting spirit, claim His promise "never to leave us nor forsake us," and resolve to begin again. Or accuse God of being the cause of our misery, become bitter and resentful toward Him and all those around us.

Christians know they are not exempt from trouble. But they know it is better to be like the man who, when asked how he managed to cope so well with his problems, answered, "Well, when life closes in on me, I tell myself that the Bible always uses the phrase, 'It came to pass.' It never says, 'It came to stay.' So I just ask God to help me be strong while the trouble is passing through." Jesus has promised to be our Shepherd and lead us Home, no

xiv Fruit from the Vine

matter what happens between now and then.

In his book, *Disappointment with God*, Phillip Yancey writes: "No matter how we rationalize, God will sometimes *seem* unfair from the perspective of a person trapped in time. Only at the end of time, after we have attained God's level of viewing, after every evil has been punished or forgiven, every illness healed, and the entire universe restored, only then will fairness reign. Then we will understand what role is played by evil, and by the Fall, and by natural law, in an 'unfair' event like the death of a child. Until then, we will not know, and can only trust in a God who does know . . . What we feel now, we will not always feel. Our disappointment is itself a sign, an aching, a hunger for something better. And faith is, in the end, a kind of homesickness—for a home we have never visited but have never stopped longing for."

When we're finally "home," our Father will "wipe every tear from our eyes. There will be no more death or mourning or crying or pain, for the old order of things has passed away" (Rev. 21:4).

Our Creator God surely thought of a good thing when He provided a way for us to release our disappointments, grief, and anger.

All of us need to cry sometimes. Counselors say that those who can cry real tears, are the ones who heal faster and are able to eventually triumph over the disappointment or loss they have suffered. God is keenly aware of all our heartaches and tears.

Are the problems and pressures you are facing getting to be too much—so much that they are threatening your faith? There are several time-tested ways of keeping your faith that you can count on, ways that have really helped me: *First,* keep your friendship with God alive, and pray daily for strength and guidance. Providing peace of mind and heart is one of His specialties. *Second,* search the Scriptures regularly for God's wise counsel and encouragement. One way is to read at least one Psalm, one Proverb, and one passage from the New Testament every day. Remember, "God is a rewarder of those who diligently seek Him" (Heb. 11:6, KJV). St. Peter also offers excellent advice: "Do you want more and more of God's kindness and peace? Then learn to know Him better and better. For as you know Him better, He will give you, through His great power, everything you need for living a truly good life . . ." (II Peter 1:2-3, TLB). *Third,* it will help keep your faith strong and ready for emergencies, if you belong to a small Christian support group in addition to an alive-and-moving church! *Fourth,* keep on reading inspirational books from which you can pick up morsels of wisdom, hope and encouragement.

If you're disappointed and mad at God about the way things are going in your life right now, don't give up on your problems yet—at least, not until you have read what all the faith-filled contributors to this book have to say. I think you will be surprised at the comfort and wisdom you will find.

Alice E. Flaherty

God of our life, there are days
  When the burdens we carry chafe our shoulders and
    weigh us down;
  When the road seems dreary and endless, the skies gray
    and threatening;
  When our lives have no music in them, and our hearts
    are lonely,
  And our souls have lost their courage.

Flood the path with light, we beseech Thee;
  Turn our eyes to where the skies are full of promise;
    To brave music.

Give us the sense of comradeship with heroes and saints
    of every age
  And so quicken our spirits that we may be able to
    encourage the
  Souls of all who journey with us on the road of life,
  To Thy honor and glory. Amen.

                                        St. Augustine

*Born in LaPorte, Indiana, David S. Handley had originally intended to be a doctor. In college he decided to become a minister, instead, and since 1981 has been senior pastor of the First Presbyterian Church in Evanston, Illinois.*

# The Silence of God in the Storms of Life

## David S. Handley

The telephone rang at 6:00 AM. My adrenalin was already going by the time I reached it. In a pastor's household, calls at that early hour nearly always mean bad news or a crisis of some kind.

A nurse from the Emergency Room at Chicago's Northwestern Memorial Hospital was calling. Could I come right over? There was a five-month-old baby girl whose life was in danger, and the mother was asking for me to come and pray with her. The mother was a friend of ours and a member of our church. Her husband was out of town on business. They had an older child, a four-year-old son, and little Elizabeth had been the joyful result of Nancy's trying many months unsuccessfully to get pregnant. Then finally, there she was—a beautiful little girl!

1

**A Whispered Prayer**

I found myself whispering a prayer as I ran the two blocks to the hospital. "God, don't let it happen; save her life, Lord!" But when I arrived at the Emergency Room it only took one look at the blank stare on the mother's face to tell me it was all over. Sudden Infant Death Syndrome. Nancy just looked at me with a lifeless despair in her eyes and said, "Thanks for coming, David. I had wanted you to say a prayer over Elizabeth, but there's no need now because she's gone."

We were ushered back into a private waiting room as we awaited all those awful questions that would have to follow. Social workers, the police, the medical staff. As we waited alone, her impassive resignation turned into a panicked denial. "David, tell me it's not true! This couldn't have happened! She was so special to us!" And then her denial finally just dissolved in tears of inconsolable grief. And all I could offer in the midst of this nightmare were two very inadequate arms to put around her and a shoulder to sob upon. I remember muttering an angry prayer to myself: "Lord, how can You expect me to defend Your ways when Your ways seem so indefensible?!" The Silence of God.

Two days later, I sat with both parents in my office at the church as we talked things through and planned the funeral service. This time it was the father's turn to weep. And as the waves of grief swept over him, in between sobs, he vented his anger and frustration at God. "I don't understand why He would let this happen. We've always tried to live good and godly lives.What's the sense in all this? I think God is being very mean!" The Silence of God.

Every Christian must experience it in one way or another; most of us (thankfully) in less dramatic ways than these two parents. A middle-aged man, laid off from his job, prays and searches for a new job; months go by without even a nibble. He experiences "the silence of God." A 39-year-old woman who has never been able to get pregnant suddenly finds she has conceived. A devout Roman Catholic, she goes twice a week to Mass and prays for that baby's life, only to have her new hopes dashed four weeks later when she miscarries. She knows "the Silence of God." A single man who for years has longed to meet the right woman and share his life with her, goes on and on with his prayers unanswered. The Silence of God.

### Life's "Curve Balls"

Life has a way of throwing some cruel curve balls, doesn't it? Yet, one thing we should note right away (though it may be very obvious to some) is that the problem of "the Silence of God" is a *believer's* problem. I have often spoken with people who are going through this dark night of the soul, who are almost apologetic. They feel quite inferior spiritually and a little bit guilty for feeling angry at God, for doubting His reality or His Goodness. But if we hadn't believed in a Good and Loving and All-Powerful God in the first place, there wouldn't be any crisis of Faith. Life's lumps would just be borne stoically. "That's Fate, that's life," we'd say, and we'd bite the bullet and move on.

But it's the Christian who has had great Faith and expectations in God, and then had those expectations dashed, who has the additional anguish of spiritual disillusionment. Yes, this kind of skepticism is a believer's skepticism. The anger is more a lover's complaint than an atheist's conviction.

The Bible is full of lovers' complaints with God. In that well-known New Testament scene at Lazarus' tomb, Mary and Martha come out to greet Jesus as He comes four days too late, and fling the accusation at Him: "Master, if you had been here, my brother would not have died!" (John 11:21,32). On the Cross, Jesus Himself cries out, "My

God, my God, why hast Thou forsaken me?" (Mark 15:34). Yes, those who are plagued by the silence of God will find much company in the Bible.

All of this is not unlike the position in which the disciples found themselves as they pulled at the oars and cursed the wind on that tempest-tossed sea. Here they were, having been blindly obedient to the Master, even though their better judgment as fishermen had told them that Jesus' instructions to cross Lake Galilee at night was very risky indeed. They knew all too well the sudden gales that could sweep across that lake at night. But they trusted Jesus, and went anyway. And, halfway across the lake, all hell broke loose!

> "A fierce gale of wind arose, and the waves beat against the boat, until it was practically filling up with water" (Mark 4:37).

### Lord, Don't You Care if We Perish?

Have you ever been in a boat out in the middle of a lake at night, when the wind really begins to whip up? It's a frightening experience. And to make matters worse, the disciples (who had been trained to look to Jesus and depend upon Him to get them through life's crises) look for the Master, and He's asleep at the switch! So the disciples come to their sleeping Lord, and can't understand His indifference to their plight. They say, "Lord, do you not *care* if we perish?" It's an indictment that was flung at Jesus by some frightened and disillusioned disciples, whose security in Christ was being shattered by the storms of life! Everything was up for grabs! "Lord! Do you not *care* if we perish?"

One of the earliest struggles I encountered with "the Silence of God" came when I was in college, a year or two after I had made the commitment of my life to Christ. I found myself in a leadership position in a couple of campus Christian groups, which meant a lot of public exposure and speaking in very secular (some would say "pagan") settings across the campus. In my young and naive Christian Faith, I maintained a very idealistic and perfectionist view of what the Christian experience was all about. A Christian, through the power of Christ, was on top of it all! No struggles; no problems; no worries. Wasn't it wonderful! Well, it *was* wonderful, this newfound Faith. But then I began to encounter severe fits of anxiety each week before I was scheduled to speak at the open campus meeting. My Thursdays would be total darkness. I would be weighed down with dread as I contemplated the meeting coming up that evening.

For months I struggled with that. The anxiety was compounded by guilt. After all, Christians weren't supposed to be anxious. Christians weren't supposed to be afraid. I prayed for deliverance, but the deliverance did not come. Finally I swallowed my pride and shared this struggle with a brother Christian whom I trusted and respected.

The picture is still etched in my memory of sitting down with him in the student union. And in a very gentle way he led me to the experience of the Apostle Paul, whose "thorn in the flesh" (whatever it was) was a constant plague to him. In his second letter to the Corinthians (12:7-10), the Apostle Paul tells us that he prayed and prayed and prayed that it be removed. But it was not. And to my amazement (and relief) I saw that Paul, too, had experienced "the Silence of God" in whatever struggle this was. And furthermore, the answer that finally came back to him from the Lord was far different than what he had asked. "My grace is sufficient for you, for *My power* is made perfect *in your weakness.*

Well, for me this was like a new lease on life. Not that I particularly relished the idea that I would likely have to go on putting up with these anxiety attacks. But that God was with me in the midst of that anxiety. Indeed, His

power could be shown even more powerfully because of
my weakness. The point to all this is that through the
experience of God's silence, when my prayers seemed to
go unanswered, when God seemed to be asleep at the oars,
it was then that I discovered a maturing of my Faith beyond
the simplistic expectations I had had before.

I believe it was out of the Nazi concentration camp
experience of Victor Frankl that these words come, which
were seen scrawled on a prison wall in the midst of the
Holocaust:

I believe in the sun,
    even when it is not shining.
I believe in love
    even when the world is
    filled with hate.
I believe in God,
    even when He is silent.

### God's Silence Doesn't Last Forever

We must remember that God's silence doesn't last forever.
Our prayers may not be answered in the way we ask them.
But eventually our prayers are answered! And we
experience "the great calm" (Mark 4:39). We've got to
believe that, friends. Christ's peace will come! And when
we begin to see God's hand moving again in specific ways,
we are likely to respond as did the disciples when a great
calm came over the sea—and they were "filled with awe"!

You see, in the end the silence of God is not dealt
with constructively by debating the *cause* of things
happening (whether it be God, human will, or chance).
Nor is the silence of God even to be dealt with finally
by speculating about the *purpose* of the trial. Rather, our
experience of the silence of God can finally be dealt with
constructively only in trust; only by *entrusting* ourselves (yes,
sometimes blindly) into the arms of God; and in that trust

wait for the cloud to lift and the sun to shine again.

Dr. Joseph Bayly, a devout Christian who lost three of his own sons to illness and accident, wrote a very moving and sensitive testimony in his book *The View from a Hearse.* He put it this way: "*Reason* gropes in the dark for answers; *Faith* waits for God." To wait expectantly, and keep on waiting, for God to deliver and bring His peace is the most purifying act of Faith that could be exercised.

"He is perfect in faith," says George MacDonald, "who can come to God in the utter dearth of his feelings and desires, without a glow of aspiration, without the weight of low thoughts, failures, neglects . . . and still say to God 'Thou art my refuge.' "

Isn't this really what the disciples did? You see, the victory of these disciples here was not that they were so full of Faith (for they were scared to death). The victory was not that they were strong-willed and kept a "stiff upper lip" through their ordeal. No!

### Victory Comes Through Trust

The victory of the disciples was that they *trusted* Jesus Christ enough to realize they could take their anger and their disillusionment and their frustration and their sense of forsakeness to Him. You know, it takes a pretty big Faith to get mad at God and say to His Son, "Teacher—do you not *care* if we perish?" And it was in the talking with Christ, even in this accusatory and angry way, that Christ's power came and Christ's peace conquered. Jesus stretched out His arms over the turbulent waters of their lives and said, "Peace! Be still! . . . And there was a great calm." The disciples had interpreted God's silence as a silence of indifference. Finally, Christ revealed it as a creative silence of *waiting,* and a prelude to an invincible Faith.

October 1979: My wife and I attended a conference in Richmond, Virginia, and on the way stopped in Arlington to see the couple who had lost their 5-month-old girl a year before. The father had since been transferred to Washington, D.C. by his law firm. As we mounted the stairs to their apartment, the memories of that nightmare at the hospital flooded my mind, and all the questions came back to me like a storm in the night.

### A New Baby Girl!

As we stood in the dark hallway and knocked at their door, suddenly the door swung open and the light in the apartment revealed Nancy's beaming face, holding a baby girl to whom she had given birth just weeks earlier. As we sat with these battle-scarred Christian friends, and looked at pictures of their baby girl who had died, and played on the floor with their newborn child, somehow we knew that the silence of God had been broken in their lives now. The cloud of doubt and despair had lifted, and the sun was shining again. God was speaking again.

No, they didn't *understand* it any better; there was no simplistic talk of "higher purpose" involved in Elizabeth's death. That remained a profound mystery and deep scar for them, and always will. But it was a wound that had now been healed over; yes, there was a scar, but it now remained as a grateful reminder of God's strengthening power in the midst of the strife—God's mysterious purpose behind this disturbing silence.

### Comforting Words from William Cowper

God moves in mysterious ways His wonders to perform;
He plants His footsteps in the sea, and rides upon the
storm.
Deep in unfathomable mines of never-failing skill
He treasures up His bright designs, and works His sovereign
will.

Ye fearful saints, fresh courage take; the clouds ye so much
    dread
Are big with mercy, and shall break in blessings on your
    head.
Blind unbelief is sure to err, and scan His work in vain;
God is His own Interpreter, and He will make it plain.
William Cowper, 1774

Let us press on in *trust,* so we may experience the fullness of Faith as it is reflected in, "I believe in God, even when He is silent."

*Father John Powell is a member of the Society of Jesus and a professor of theology at Loyola University in Chicago. A best-selling author, his books have sold in the millions.*

# Turn Off Those Worry Faucets

## John Powell

Did you hear about the two little birds that were flying over the earth? They looked down at people who had worried expressions on their faces, asking themselves, "Am I going to have enough? Am I going to have enough of this, enough of that?" One of the little birds said to the other, "Apparently, they don't know that they have a Heavenly Father who cares for them."

We know the truth behind this little story, but we still hate it, don't we, when someone says, "Don't worry"? I always want to say to someone who tells me that: "If worry were a faucet, I would turn it off." But it's not a faucet, is it?

I have a friend, a teacher, who claims that worry really helps. He says, "Don't tell me worry doesn't help. Everything I've ever worried about hasn't come true." However, he goes through life with a semi-terrified look on his face. One day his class put an anonymous note on his desk, which read, "If you feel all right, would you please notify your face?"

We have to face the fact, as Christians, that Jesus was big on *not* worrying. "Look at the lilies of the field and the birds in the air," He says. "They don't have to worry. Neither do you."

Remember Jesus' friend Martha? (She was something of a twitch.) She comes out of the kitchen complaining that her sister Mary isn't doing enough to help. Jesus says something like, "Oh, Martha, honey, you get so upset about so many things and most of them are small. Only one thing is necessary, my dear—one thing: trust. Put your trust in Me. I will be your *enough.*"

And remember the old salts of the sea? We call them the Twelve Apostles. They're out in a boat with Jesus. After a hard day, Jesus is lying in the bottom of the boat, resting, when a storm comes up. Suddenly, those old salty sailors start waking Jesus. "Master, Master! Does it not concern you that we could drown?" Jesus stands up, wipes the sleep out of His eyes, and raises His hands. There comes a great calm. Then He turns to His followers and says, "Why are you worried? Don't you know that I am with you?" He asks us the same question, and He adds, "Don't you know that I love you?"

## My Practice and My Preaching

I have to admit, to be thoroughly honest, that my own practice does not come up to my preaching. I was recently on a speaking tour in New Zealand, in an area where there are chemical smelters that melt down chemicals and give off an acrid, smoky odor. I was preaching to a group of perhaps 600 people, and I had them in the palm of my hand. To emphasize my theme that worry is a form of atheism, I was telling the story of Jesus calming the sea and asking his disciples, "Why are you worried?" Suddenly, my nostrils started tweaking. I smelled smoke. A panicky look came over my face, and I said, "Excuse me. Do you smell smoke?"

Someone answered, "It's the chemical smelters. They give off that odor. There's no fire."

My mouth had been saying, "Why are you worried?" but my face betrayed my fear. Some wag in the back called out, "Why are you worried?"

Though I don't always practice what I preach, I truly believe what I preach. Most of me, that is. My mouth believes it, and my head believes it. Sometimes my stomach doesn't. I really don't like it when people tell me, "Don't worry." Then I have to face Jesus, who says the same thing. "Don't worry." I think I would be a little upset with *him* except that he tells us what to do with our worries: "Look at the lilies of the field and the birds of the air. I'll take care of all your daily needs. You make the Kingdom of God your primary concern" (based on Luke 12:22-34).

Psychologists call this *sublimation.* Imagine yourself as a cylinder. Coming through the cylinder that is you is a quantified amount of psychic energy. You have a certain precise amount. You are equipped with handles that you can turn on or off. You can let a trickle of your psychic energy out, or you can let a great gush come out. The point is: *You can adjust the flow.*

What Jesus is saying is, "Don't let your energy—your strength—trickle out of trivia. Don't worry about what you're going to eat or wear. I will be your *enough* and take care of you. Turn off all the little spigots of worry, and direct your strength to the Kingdom. All your little worries will die of neglect."

### Who's Going to Push Our Wheelchairs?

An old priest friend of mine comes into my room occasionally. He is a worrier.He paces back and forth in my room as I follow his movements from my swivel chair—something like a tennis game. He keeps saying, "We've taken vows of poverty. We don't have any money in the bank. Who's going to push our wheelchairs?" I'm always tempted to say, "Do not worry about what you will eat, or what you will wear, or who will push your wheelchair. 'I will be your *enough*,' Jesus says. Direct all your energy to the Kingdom of God."

There are many examples of sublimation in our society. The artist sublimates. He doesn't really care what he's wearing—maybe blue jeans and an old sloppy sweatshirt. He has a vision of beauty inside himself, and he's trying to share that inner beauty with the world. It's all he thinks about. He eats, sleeps, and breathes his art. It's all that really matters to him.

Sometimes we see sublimation in a scientist, someone like Thomas Edison. He slept only three hours a night, with little cat naps in between his inventions. All of his energy was directed to them.

Sometimes we see sublimation in the politician, especially at election time. He says, "Get that vote! How many counties have we heard from?" It's all he thinks about. He directs all his energy into his campaign.

**Direct Your Energy to the Kingdom of God**

Jesus tells us to direct all our energy to the Kingdom of God. Don't let worry trickle out on trivia. Don't sit on the curbstone of life having an identity crisis, asking "Who's going to hold my hand?" Get out there and love! Ask yourself at all the moments of decision in your life: What is the loving thing to do? Then do that. All those little worries—all those little parasites that crawl inside our souls—will die. They will all die of neglect if you make your life an act of love.

Let the Kingdom of God be your primary concern. What

is the Kingdom of God? All Scripture scholars agree that the Kingdom of God is the central message of Jesus. They don't agree on what the Kingdom means, however. I would like to suggest that the description of the Kingdom Jesus is talking about is an invitation from God. Our God says to us, "I love you. Will you please come to Me? Come to Me because I love you." The invitation isn't extended to the individual but to all of us. So I can't say yes to God without saying yes to *you*. I can't love God unless I love you. Unless you love me, you can't really say yes to God. The French poet Charles Peguy wrote, "Don't ever try to go to God alone, because He will certainly ask you an embarrassing question: 'Where are your brothers and sisters? Didn't you bring them with you?' "

So the Kingdom of God is an invitation to all of us to come to God in love. He says, "I have always loved you. Before the world was made, I knew you and loved you. You've always been a part of my mind and heart. I could not have made the world without you. Any world without you would be incomplete."

This is good news, isn't it? God tells us, "I love you. I have always loved you. You don't have to win or earn or be worthy of my love. It's a gift. It's a given. You don't have to change so I will love you. You need to understand that I do love you so that you *can* change." God is inviting us to come to Him in love, to say yes to one another and to come to Him together as His children.

**Jesus Says, "Trust Me"**

Jesus said, "Let this be your primary concern, and I will take care of all your other daily needs. *Trust Me.* When the questions arise, 'Will I have enough?' remember I will be your *enough.* Let the Kingdom of God be your primary concern."

It's really harder to love on Monday morning than on

Sunday, yet this is what He calls us to do. "If you make love your primary concern," He says, "I promise you I will take care of everything else." Our prayer should be, "Lord, help me to say yes to your invitation to the Kingdom of love, to say the yes of love to my brothers and sisters. Help me to make that the rule and the motive of my life."

There are no strangers in my world, only brothers and sisters, some of whom I haven't met yet. They have needs. Some of them are starving. Some of them are lonely. Some of them are twisting in pain. Some of them comb through garbage cans to find the food to stay alive. Some regard the discards of others as their treasures. Some know only the joy of cheap wine and the sting of a hypodermic needle. I must say yes to loving them, and yet I must also love myself. I must make a judgment about what is the loving thing to do. I have to confront each of my brothers and sisters. I have to study them, empathize with them, get out of myself and into them and ask: "What do you need? What do you need me to be? I want to be that for you. What do you need me to say? I will say it. What is the loving thing to do?"

Sometimes love asks me to be tough. You're an alcoholic, and I love you too much to watch you destroy yourself. You must do something about this. Love sometimes must be tender. When you sit in the dark room of failure, let me sit silently at your side. What do you need? I want to be that for you. I want to love you. It's not always easy to know what the loving thing to do is. Jesus does not hold us responsible for being infallible in this matter. Sometimes we make mistakes and we must learn through them. What He asks is this: "Make love your primary concern. Be sure that whatever you do is an act of love. And even when you knock things over, I'll be walking next to you and I'll straighten them up."

**Let Love Be the Rule of Your Life**

During the Last Supper, Jesus tells the Twelve Apostles to make love the rule of their lives. He tells them—and us: "If you do this, I promise that you will be very happy. If the question that throbs inside you is, 'What will I wear?' or, 'How will I look?' or, 'Who's going to push my wheelchair?' you'll miss the blessing. If the only question you ask is, 'What is the loving thing to do?' then you're going to be happy, and peace will be My gift to you. When all the other questions arise in you—the anxious questions, the nervous questions—remember that the answer to all of them is the same. Trust Me. Make the Kingdom of God your primary concern. I love you. I will be with you. I will take care of you. Whenever you ask, 'Will I have enough?' remember I will be your *enough*."

*A native of New York City, Woodie W. White grew up in Harlem, and was elected Resident Bishop of the Central and Southern Illinois Conferences of the United Methodist Church in 1984. Eight years later, he became Bishop of the Indiana Area.*

# Keep On Singing the Song

## Woodie W. White

"Sing a song," the psalmist wrote, "Oh, sing a song. Sing a song, for God has done marvelous things." The book of Psalms is one of my favorites because it seems to have a message for every occasion, whether it be one of joy or sadness. I can always find something in Psalms that speaks eloquently to my needs.

It is said that in Europe there is a little bird called the chaffinch, a bird that is very popular and purchased by the thousands. It looks very much like our male robin, yet it sings like a canary. Many people buy this bird for their home, only to discover that it has a very peculiar characteristic. Unlike the canary, the chaffinch can forget how to sing. The owner must take it back into the woods two or three times a year so it can hear other chaffinches sing. If it does not hear other chaffinch birds singing, it will mope and mope and eventually die, because it has forgotten how to sing.

That might be a message for the church. If we forget how to sing the Good News of Jesus Christ, we will mope, loose our way, and in fact, we too might die.

There is a scene in the play, *A Raisin in the Sun,* I'll never forget. The story centers around a family that is held together by "Mama," a very strong-willed woman. In one scene Mama is talking with her young daughter, a sophomore in college. The daughter feels she has discovered "so much" about life. She says, "Mama, there is no such thing as God."

Slowly, Mama moves to her daughter and asks, "Child, what did you say?"

The daughter repeats, "There is no such thing as God."

With that, Mama slaps her daughter across the face and says, "Repeat after me: 'In my mother's house there is still God.' "

The world often acts as if there is no God. We live in a world of inexplicable suffering, pain, and disaster. The earth shakes, buildings crumble, the innocent die, children go hungry. We live in a world of racism and sexism. We live in a world of classism. We live in a world of deep sin. We live in a world where people shout, "There is no God!"

Those who know there *is* a God must be able to sing of that fact so the world may hear the song and respond to it. Sing the song! Has the church forgotten how to sing about her faith, and about the message that Jesus is real?

We must not forget how to sing. The world needs to hear our song—a song of love, a song of faith, a song of justice. When the world listens to our song, heartache becomes less of an ache, and the sense of lostness is replaced with a sense of hope. We must learn how to sing again so that those who desperately need to hear the song will hear it from those who know it.

I once received a note from a church member that read, "I met the Lord Jesus 65 years ago, and I've been singing

a song ever since." I pray that we will sing such a song
for those who need to hear it. Sing the song! Sing it when
you are alone, when you are burdened, and when the night
is long. Sing the song when you are up and joyful. Sing
the song when it seems as if you can't make it one day
longer. Sing the song even when you don't feel like singing,
and the song will become something you will marvel at.

Those of us who have had the song put in our hearts
know what it does for life. When you are lost, or confused,
you know that somehow the Lord brings hope and life
and justice. So sing the song. Sing the song to the Lord,
for He has done marvelous things. Sing the song when
times seem unbearable and life unfair. Sing the song!

I was born in the heart of Harlem—like many of my
peers a wayward youth, moving in the wrong direction.
But it was there that someone sang the song to me in
a way that I could understand. If I had not heard the song,
I would never have known the Lord Jesus.

She was a tough teacher. She gave me a hard time. She
seemed to pick on me. She was Southern. She was white.
She had the worst drawl I ever heard. Yet I discovered
that this college teacher knew the song. And she sang it
to me in such a way that I could no longer see color or
class, or distinctions of gender. She was able to show me
something I had missed before: Beauty goes far beyond
physical attraction. We are all broader than our nation or
race. Loyalty, ultimate loyalty, is to Jesus alone. This teacher
came into my life and sang a song that eventually changed
me. My life will never be the same.

So now I must sing the song—sing it wherever I go,
even when I don't feel like it. Because in the singing I
have discovered the power of Jesus to change the lowly
and the lonely, the lost and fearful, even those filled with
prejudice and malice. The power of Jesus makes us new,
and helps us understand the meaning of His life, death
and resurrection.

Let us sing to this world of brokenness and division. Let us sing to this world of confusion in which we seem to want to destroy ourselves. Let us sing to those who desperately need to hear the song. And in the singing, someone may ask, "What is the Source of your song?" Then we can point to the Source. It is not us, nor our strength, nor our intelligence, nor our ingenuity. We must point to the Source of our singing, which is Jesus Christ, and share Him with those who are lost, lonely, frightened, and filled with torment. They need to hear the song.

Won't those of you who know the song sing it? Sing it in your office. Sing it in your living room. Sing it on the campus. Sing it on the farm. Sing it even when you don't feel like singing it. And soon the Source of your singing will touch and change the world, and you will never be the same because you sang the song—the song of Jesus and His love. Sing the song!

*For more than 35 years, Oswald C. J. Hoffmann has served as a pastor, college professor, and speaker for "The Lutheran Hour," the popular Christian radio program originating in St. Louis, and heard around the world in some 45 languages.*

# Forgive, Forget— and Live Again!

## Oswald C. J. Hoffmann

We live in a world of sin. We just have to face that fact. I know we are not supposed to talk about sin anymore. Some people say that's "God talk" and avoid it. At Hubert Humphrey's funeral, after everybody else had spoken, the President of the United States, Jimmy Carter, got up and said that he and Hubert Humphrey had once talked for an entire evening at Camp David about sin. It is a remarkable thing when people reach the practicality of life and come to that great moment when they face death, they talk about something real. Sin!

I have noticed that you don't have to convince children of the fact that there is anything like sin in the world. When I ask children, "Do you know about sin?"—they usually say, "Yeah, we know all about that." It's their parents you have to convince that there is something like sin. They have more or less ruled it out of their consciousness. But sin is one of those things that is around us all the time.

21

When we recognize that fact, we begin to see life as it really is. I have an old friend who used to be a Congressman. Some years ago he was defeated. He said that he left Congress "with the consent of the electorate." Even at the age of 80, he still had his sense of humor. He told me about his pastor talking to his congregation about sin. He said, "Of course, there is no one here who has never committed a sin, and I dare say there is nobody here who even knows of anyone who has never committed a sin. Just to make sure, let's ask if there is anybody here who has never committed a sin. If there is, let him or her stand up." Nobody stood up, of course, except for one fellow in the back. The pastor fixed his eye on him and said, "You mean to tell me you have never committed a sin in your whole life?" The man answered, "No, I'm not standing up for myself. I'm standing up for my wife's first husband."

Sometimes humor tells us a great deal about our humanity. There are people who deny that there is anything like sin in the world, yet they will laugh at that joke, because they know there isn't anyone in this world of ours who hasn't sinned.

## Jesus Paid the Price—for Us

Then Jesus came into the world. One of His men said, "He was made to be sin for us." What a remarkable thing! That is plain talk, but it is also a tremendous fact. It is true that He, the Son of God, became an ordinary human like us. That is why He did it—in order that He might be made sin for us. The whole Gospel is in those two little words, "for us."

He took our sin into His own body on that piece of wood on which He was crucified and died. Sin and death go together. For the life of me, I don't see how one can ever talk at a funeral without bringing up the subject of

sin, which is what made it what it is. I don't know how
anyone can have any hope on such an occasion without
talking about Jesus Christ and what God did for us through
Him. Christ died and took our sins into His own body
on the Cross, so that henceforth we might make a clean
break with sin and be found in Him. That is forgiveness.
When God looks at Christ, He sees everyone who is in
Christ. That is the good word of the Gospel.

### Our Only Hope

The only hope any of us have is that we might be found
in Him when God looks at us. That is the purpose of Christ
in this world. The Bible tells us, "Though He was God
in every way, nevertheless He took upon Himself the form
of a bond-servant; being found in fashion as a man, He
humbled Himself, became obedient unto death—the death
of a common criminal on a cross. For that, God gave Him
a name that would be above every name—so that every
knee should bow . . . and every tongue confess that Jesus
Christ is Lord to the glory of God the Father" (Philippians
2:7-11).

That Gospel does something for people. It brings them
to life again. I guess the great story is that He didn't lie
there in the grave. You aren't going to find His bones
there as you would of every other great person in history.
No, He was raised from the dead by the glory of His Father,
and declared to be the Son of God with power by
resurrection from the dead. That is the good news the
apostles went out to tell people. Of course, people found
it difficult to believe in those days just as they do today.
I can imagine what people must have said when the apostles
first went out to tell them about how Jesus Christ had been
raised from the dead. Jesus Christ,—the Jesus they knew,
and saw, and had talked and eaten with.

When people scoffed at the idea, the apostles said, "But

we *saw* Him, and we can't help but tell you the things we *saw* and *heard*." That is the gospel.

People "saw" Him too, even though they had not seen Him in the same way the apostles did, but "saw" Him through their words and began to understand and come to life again, too. That is why St. Peter said, "Hurray for God!" I am translating that literally now: "Hurray for God, the Father of our Lord Jesus Christ, who out of the magnificence of His mercy *has brought us to life again* and given us a hope that is alive through the resurrection of Jesus Christ from the dead."

## One Hope That Never Dies

It is not like all those other hopes that have died. There have been plenty of them, haven't there—even in this century? For example, the hope that we would reorganize life and bring things back again just through organization. People were going to organize biology; they were going to organize physics which everybody thought was dead until World War II; and they were going to organize humanity. Then finally, when we were all through, we would have everything organized and everything would be beautiful.

Well, all you have to do is look at the world today, and you can see that organization hasn't done very much for us. In fact, it has only helped to confuse the whole thing. Maybe we are more chaotic today than we ever were with all of our organization. Maybe we have begun to realize, too, what it is to have God active and caring. The good news of the Gospel is that *He cares!* We see it in Jesus Christ. He cares enough to bring people to life again and to help them realize how good it is to live again. He does that in a very ordinary way—by forgiveness.

That is also hard to believe: that anyone could forgive. I know people will say, "I can forgive, but I can't forget." That's not forgiveness. That's just layin' for 'em. When God forgives, He forgives *and forgets,* "As far as east is from the west, so far has He removed our transgressions from us" (Psalm 103:12, KJV).

## A Great Act of Faith

It happened one day when the Lord was teaching as He so often did, with a big crowd around, that four young men (young engineers) brought a friend of theirs who was ill and laid out on a mat. They had to be engineers to manage this thing, to keep the fellow from falling off the mat during their long and arduous trip. But when they arrived, they found they couldn't get in the house where Jesus was. So they carried out another great act of faith. They put their engineering minds to work and managed to get him up onto the roof, again without his falling off the mat. Then they performed an even greater act of faith. They cut a hole in the roof of the house. No doubt they had a "foreman" saying, "A little bit more this way, a little more that way." When they finally got it all set up, they cut the hole big enough to let the whole mat down, not folded up, you understand, but the whole mat with the paralyzed man on it. They hit it right on the nose. They let the mat down right where Jesus was standing.

You can imagine how people below must have felt when they saw the roof open up in front of them and watched that mat being lowered by those four stalwart young men. When Jesus saw the man on the mat, He said to him, "Son, take heart, your sins are forgiven you." That, of course, wasn't what the four friends had expected. They had brought their friend because they wanted him to be healed. But the first thing Jesus said was, "Your sins are forgiven you."

Even in this last half of the 20th century, we are still being told that physical healing is the greatest good anybody can have—the greatest thing God can do for anyone. Don't

you believe it! God can heal people from the inside out.
He can do things that are even greater than that. He can
turn death itself into life. We have seen it in His Son, and
we have seen it in the lives of people, too—just like coming
back from death to life, "out of darkness into light and
a new life again." It is through forgiveness that this happens,
and it is in His Son.

### Not By Religion—But By Faith

By the way, there were some nice religious people around
who said, "Who can forgive sins but God only?" They were
right—who can? But Jesus knew why they asked that
question. There are always religious people who know better
than anybody else. I have never noticed anyone who was
saved by religion. I have seen a lot of people saved by
faith, but not by religion and the little pieties that we have.
Jesus said, "What in the world ever made you say a thing
like that? Which is easier to say, 'your sins are forgiven
you' or to say, 'get up and walk'? That you may know that
the Son of Man has power on earth to forgive sin." Then
Jesus told the young man on the mat to take up his bed
and go home. So that's just what he did.

He got up, picked up his mat and went home, rejoicing
and praising God. That is the way the Gospel is—very direct
and simple.

There is only one other thing about it! Even though
some of the Jewish religious leaders thought it was
blasphemy for Jesus to say He could forgive sin, the people
were struck with awe and wonder at what they had witnessed.
They not only had heard Jesus tell the young man that
his sins were forgiven, but they saw a miracle of physical
healing as well.

That is how He transforms the lives of people here and
now, and how He transforms them in the life that is to
be. "Death—where is your sting?" Death has a sting. Why

should anyone be afraid of a swarm of hornets? Because of their sting, that's why! If you pulled the "sting" from all those hornets, you wouldn't have to worry about them. They would be no more harmful than houseflies. That is what God has done with death. He has pulled the "sting," and turned it into something that nobody every dreamed it could be. He had turned death itself into life! "O Death, where is your sting?"

"The sting of death is sin, and the strength of sin is the law, but thanks be to God who gives us the victory through our Lord Jesus Christ" (I Cor. 15:56-57).

## How Do You Recognize Faith?

The way you recognize faith is in the way people express themselves in love toward one another. I spoke on a college campus recently in eastern Tennessee. I was speaking about the resurrection of Christ and how people get new life from knowing that He is the Lord of Heaven and earth. I had been told earlier that there was a young man in their midst who had been diagnosed with terminal cancer. His name was Eddie. He was soon to go to New York for an operation on a very difficult and sensitive cancer. When I referred to his situation, someone pointed to him. So I asked him if he would like to come up and say a few words to his friends. He did not hesitate to respond. There he stood, and without any preparation at all, this is what he said to all the young people in the audience: "I want to thank you for the love you have surrounded me with. Many of you don't know me because I'm a freshman. But I just want you to know how much it means to me that you love me and are concerned about me." He went on to talk about his faith—and about their faith. He closed his remarks by saying, "Thanks for all the love you have given me."

I stood there for 45 minutes afterwards while hundreds

of students came up, embraced Eddie, whispered a little comfort into his ear, and went on. A lot of the girls were crying openly, and young men walked off solemn-faced. I said to myself, "This is life."

I know why those young people were doing what they did. They know something—they know Someone. They were taking to heart what the apostle Paul said, "Thanks be to God, who gives us the victory through our Lord-raised-from-the-dead" (I Cor. 15:57).

So being the people we are, let's be firm. Let's be unmoved. Let's be overflowing with love, doing the Lord's work here on earth, in whatever vocation we happen to be. Let us remember that nothing done with faith and love toward the Lord is ever futile.

*Lloyd John Ogilvie, senior pastor of the First Presbyterian Church of Hollywood, California, is the author of numerous books about the Christian faith. He can be seen on Sunday mornings, on the television program "Let God Love You," emanating from his church.*

# Be A First Stepper!

## Lloyd J. Ogilvie

There is a delightful New Year's Eve custom in Scotland called "first-footing it." The idea is to be the first person to step across a friend's threshold to wish him "Happy New Year" and toast his health and happiness.

I want to build on that tradition in establishing what might be called "The Happy Fellowship of Initiative Reconcilers." The only qualification necessary is that we be willing to take the first step. We all want to be first in something. This is our chance! We can be first-stepping peacemakers.

Our motto could be Jesus' challenging seventh Beatitude: "Blessed are the peacemakers, for they shall be called sons of God." The various translations of the Beatitude shed penetrating light on the meaning. The New English Version has it, "How blest are the peacemakers; God shall call them sons of God!" J. B. Phillips renders it, "Happy are those who make peace, for they will be known as the sons of God!" William Barclay's incisive translation is, "Blessed are those who produce right relationships in every sphere of life, for they are doing a God-like work." (*The Beatitudes and the Lord's Prayer for Everyman.* New York: Harper and Row, 1975, p. 100) My own study has resulted in something like this: "Happy are the initiative enablers of peace with God, themselves, and others, for they are the kin of God in the healing of the wounds of the world." However you put it, the impact of the Beatitude is the same. We are called to receive the peace of Christ and to take the initiative in sharing it in life's relationships and responsibilities.

## Who Should Take the First Step?

*The difficulty is in taking the first step.* The old saying is true: the longest journey begins with the first step. It is not easy to go first in expressing forgiveness or seeking reconciliation. A woman said to me recently, "Why should I go to her? She hurt me! Let *her* take the first step." She missed the joy of being a first-stepper. A man confessed, "I'm filled with resentment and I'm depressed. I resent people, my job, and what life has dealt me." I tried to share that his inverted anger was causing the depression. We talked about the people he resented. "Why not go to them and talk out how you feel? Find out the causes of the broken relationships. Seek forgiveness where you're wrong and give forgiveness where you've been wronged." His response excluded him from being a first-stepper. "Why should I do that? I'm the one they should come to." I replied, "Would you forgive them and make peace if they did?" He was not ready for that question nor for the cost of the answer.

None of us finds it easy to be an initiator in making peace. It is a demanding, soul-stretching responsibility our Lord has given us. We cannot do it without Him. He is the patron of the first-steppers, and patron means pattern and defender. What He guides, He provides!

Peace is a key word of Jesus' life and ministry. He came to establish it, His message explained it, His death purchased it, and His resurrected presence enables it. The messianic predictions were that He would be the Prince of Peace (Isa. 9:6). The angels who announced His birth sang, "On earth, peace, good will toward men!" (Luke 2:14). His persistent word of absolution to sinners was, "Go in peace!" Just before He was crucified, the Lord's last will and testament was, "Peace I leave with you, My peace I give to you; not as the world gives do I give to you. Let not your heart be troubled, neither let it be afraid" (John 14:27). When the Lord returned after the resurrection, His first word to the disciples was "Shalom." Peace. The life of Jesus was saturated with His mission to bring the peace of God and to initiate the healing relationships of peace with God.

The early church was the original chapter of the "Holy Order of First Steppers." They were distinguished by the peace they received, shared, and preached. "Preaching peace by Jesus Christ" is the testimony of their central calling in Acts 10:36.

Paul opened and closed his letters with the word *peace.* No wonder! It described his own profound experience and liberating conviction. "Therefore, having been justified by faith, we have peace with God through our Lord Jesus Christ" (Rom. 5:1). The sure test of whether we have accepted the Lord's initiative love is if we know lasting peace. The Hebrew word *shalom* meant perfect welfare, serenity, fulfillment, freedom from trouble, and liberation from anything which hinders contentment. But it was not until Paul met Christ and was filled with Him that he discovered a peace which was completely unassailable by trouble. He found peace in trouble, not freedom from trouble.

### Peace *With* Christ Ushers in the Peace *of* Christ

A true first-stepper has discovered that peace with Christ ushers us into the peace of Christ. The enmity and strife are over. Separation and fear are gone. Christ, the original first-stepper, has stepped into our hearts with forgiveness and acceptance even when we did not deserve it.

Peace is a sure sign that Christ has taken up residence in us. From within, he assures us that nothing can make Him stop loving us. He has settled our destiny on the cross. Paul knew that and wrote, "For it pleased the Father that in Him all fullness should dwell, and by Him to reconcile all things to Himself, by Him, whether things on earth or things in heaven, having made peace through the blood of His cross" (Col. 1:19-20).

When we share that bold conviction, we can allow "the peace of God to rule in our hearts" (Col. 3:15). The word for "rule" in Greek is "umpire." He calls the shots and keeps us from anything which would rob us of the peace He tried to give us. He guards our hearts with His peace. "Be anxious for nothing, but in everything by prayer and supplication, with thanksgiving, let your requests by made known to God, and the peace of God, which surpasses all understanding, will guard your hearts and minds through Christ Jesus" (Phil. 4:6-7). Peace will be protector and guide. It will settle our jangled nerves, and in the midst of conflict and confusion, give us the assurance that will work together for good because the Lord is in charge. That's the gift we are given to become first-steppers.

But we cannot give what is not real to us. Peacemaking begins with an experience of peace in our own hearts. When we have received the gift of peace, we know an ordered and harmonious functioning unity, wholeness, a being knit together. That is what happens when the character implant of Christ in us takes place. The fruit of the Spirit is ours. "The fruit of the Spirit . . . is peace" (Gal. 5:22).

❧

## Make Peace With Yourself First!

Our first step as peacemaker is toward ourselves. Most of us find it difficult to initiate peace with others because we are not at peace with the person who lives in our own skin. We need to meet that unique person inside. Often we are harder on that person than anyone else. We find it difficult to forgive ourselves, even after we've heard and accepted the forgiveness of the cross. But it is blasphemy to contradict the Lord because He has loved us unreservedly. We need to ask Him to help us love ourselves as much as He does. That alone will free us of self-condemnation, negation and lambasting. A test of our acceptance of ourselves as Christ-loved and forgiven persons will be abiding peace. A profound center of calm is the result of creative delight and enjoyment of ourselves. Happy are the peacemakers—with themselves.

The natural overflow of that inner peace will be a transformed attitude toward the people around us. Then we can become initiating peacemakers with others. That first-stepping ministry has three parts: making peace between us and others; between people we know who are separated from one another because of the misunderstanding, hurt and hatred; and between groups in our society. Paul gives us marching orders for all three: "Therefore, let us pursue the things which make for peace" (Rom. 14:19).

## Before You Take That First Step

Think of the broken relationships of your life. With whom are you at odds? For whom do you continue to hold grudges or memories of hurts? Whom have you harmed or distressed whose forgiveness you need to seek? Take an incisive inventory. List the names and the memories. Happiness awaits action! A letter, a phone call, a visit— a first step. If we know of anything for which we need to share our feelings with a person who has wronged us, make this a "Do it now!" day. Knowing what unresolved tensions do to our peace of mind and our health, it is an act of self-esteem and preservation not to wait. Do it for Christ . . . do it for yourself.

I find it crucial to talk to the Lord about what I've done or what other people have done to me before I talk with them. It gives me perspective and tenderness. The Lord helps me see the deeper needs in the relationship and what has caused the problem. He also shows me myself and what I have done and said. His forgiveness provides a fresh experience of grace for my first-stepping reconciliation. He helps me imagine how to act and what to say. When I surrender the conflict to the Lord, the tension is released and I can accept my calling to be a channel of peace. A peacemaker does not "make" peace; that has already been done on the cross. Our calling is to appropriate and mediate the peace of Christ in the specific relationship that has been fractured by us or others.

The one thing we can say with certainty about our feelings is they are ours. We may be wrong or confused, but we still feel strongly. Our task as first-stepping reconcilers is to express our feelings in a way that does not make others defensive. The best way to do that is to own our feelings and express our need to be honest about how we feel. Rather than attacking, our responsibility is to tell the other person simply and clearly about how what has happened has made us feel. Often our feelings can be transformed by talking and sharing graciously.

If we need that emotional cleansing, so do others. The first-stepper is sensitive and aware. With the Spirit's imputed empathy, we will be able to see and feel when someone has feelings which need to be shared. Love demands our initiative effort to provide an opportunity for communication and an ambience of acceptance. When people know that our love is unqualified and unconditional, they will be liberated to talk until they know they are understood. A peacemaker can quickly admit whatever he or she has done or said which has caused pain. When we are falsely accused, we can share that we can imagine how the person feels and then share the situation in question from our perspective. *Reconciliation is more crucial than being right!* When Christ is present, He leads people to a new beginning. The past can be forgotten. The miracle of healing will be His gift.

### How to Help Others Become "First-Steppers"

Now we need to consider our calling to be first-steppers where conflict exists between people. The peacemaker can hear both sides without taking sides. Loving is listening. Enabling questions help. Encouragement is expressed when we tell people we understand how they feel. That does not mean that we agree or that we add fuel to the fires of their angers or hostilities.

After we have heard both people, our next initiative is to encourage direct confrontation. Offer to arrange it and to be a moderator and mediator. Something like this needs to be said: "You have told me how you feel. It is not important that I agree or disagree. I appreciate how you are feeling. But now you need to talk directly to this person. *You'll not be free until you do.* Don't put it off. You are too valuable to Christ to allow these feelings to fester. Love Him and yourself enough to deal with this broken relationship."

All this is dependent on our having earned the right to be reconcilers. That comes from deep trust and confidentiality. It is also nurtured by our openness about how Christ has helped us when we have known the pain of being misunderstood or misused. The sharing of our experiences will free the persons we are trying to help to deal with their feelings. We become fellow-sufferers rather than aloof arbitrators.

**Prayer Will Be Your Secret Ally**

*Prayer is the inner power of the peacemaker.* The Lord wants reconciliation more than we do. He will show us each step of the healing. Prayer begins with Him. He calls us into conversation to give us the gifts of wisdom, discernment, and healing. Pray before, during, and after. One of the most effective ways to help people breakthrough to new attitudes and willingness is to pray with them. Pray with each person involved in the conflict and then pray with both or all of them together. When people ask the Lord for reconciliation, the barriers begin to come down. Often little more than a prayer for the will to be willing is the beginning of healing.

Our ministry of reconciliation between groups is equally demanding. It requires that we be captured by neither group. Our challenge is to become the bridge over the troubled, turbulent waters which divide the groups. That means we must have credibility with both groups, without losing our integrity. Conflict is usually caused by power struggles. The unspoken question is "Who's in charge here?" It implies the desire to control. So many lofty theological battles and congregational schisms are simply battles for control. The peacemaker dares to ask both groups. "What is the real issue beneath the lofty rhetoric? What if we loved Christ with all our hearts, and wanted His peace more than victory? We cannot be separated from one another without eventually being separated from the Lord. What does His love demand?"

Groups are usually the reflection of strong leaders. Often the cause of conflict between groups is the bruised or slighted egos of these leaders. Our peacemaking will demand a combination of sensitivity and incisive honesty. There will be times of boldness when we must confront people with what they are doing to themselves and others. When division persists, eventually we must "speak the truth in love." And we are never alone. The indwelling power of the Lord who is our peace will guide us. Not only will He lead us each step of the way, He will also be at work in those we are trying to help. When we least expect it, He will change the impossible situation. Trust Him!

A vital credential of a peacemaker is freedom from gossip. Nothing disqualifies us in being reconcilers more than talking *about* people rather than talking *to* them. The old Spanish proverb is on target. "Whoever gossips *to* you will gossip *of* you." Relationships are strained and guarded when we are not absolutely trustable. When we gossip about others, always the question can linger of what we will say about them. A peacemaker never says anything about another person that he has not first said to that person directly. After that, why tell anyone else?

### The Peacemaker's Reward

The reward of a peacemaker is to be called a son of God. There is no greater joy for parents than to have their children want to be like them. God has made us sons and daughters to reproduce His character in us. The last part of the Beatitude gives us the secret source of our strength to be peacemakers. God is an initiator. He came in Christ. He loves us before we respond, forgives us before we ask to be forgiven, blesses us even when we are undeserving. And when we accept our status as His cherished, beloved children, we begin to grow in His likeness. We shall be like Him in spreading peace. Paul shared this same secret with the Corinthians. "Become complete. Be of good comfort, be of one mind, live in peace; and the God of love and peace will be with you" (II Cor. 13:11). In other words, if we want to know God,we must join Him in what He is doing.

Jesus called for action. Obedience is the key that unlocks the resources of His Spirit. "If you know these things, happy are you if you do them" (John 13:17). Hearing and doing are inseparable.

William James underlined the crucial relationship between hearing and action. He reminded us that no matter how full a reservoir of truths we may possess and however good our sentiments may be, if we have not taken advantage of every concrete opportunity to act, our character will remain entirely unaffected. "A character is a completely fashioned will," says James. It is a compilation of tendencies to act in a specific and decisive way. These tendencies become permanently ingrained in proportion to the frequency in which we follow through with action. When a resolve or an opportunity is neglected or refused without action, it works to hinder our future capacity to implement what we believe. Our growth in our sonship is dependent on being first-steppers in the adventure of peacemaking. To delay it or neglect it today will make it more difficult tomorrow. Why not now?

The other day on a flight across the country, I had an amazing conversation with a man seated next to me. I was busy collecting and writing down my thoughts on this seventh Beatitude. Out of the corner of my eye, I noticed his interest in what I was doing. Finally he interrupted, asking what I was working on so intently. "I'm writing the charter for a new organization," I replied playfully. "A what?" he exclaimed. "What is it called?" I smiled and said, "The Holy Order of First-Steppers!" That started a long conversation about initiative peacemaking. I shared much of what I have written here. "That's not easy," he said. We talked about the difficulties of being a reconciler. The thing he returned to repeatedly was the idea of expressing and seeking forgiveness. I knew a raw nerve had been touched in him.

When the plane landed in Chicago, he prepared to get off. "Where to now?" I asked. "Home . . . to be a first-stepper," he replied. He went on to tell me about a tragic breakdown of communication with his wife. Few words and no affection had been given for months. He told me that he had been determined not to be the first to resolve the tension because he had felt his wife was wrong. Now he knew it was his move; he was responsible to take the first step.

We shook hands. "Power to you, first-stepper!" I said. "And to you!" he replied with new joy.

*Dr. Bruce Larson is co-pastor of the famed Crystal Cathedral, in Garden Grove, California. Born and reared in Chicago, after graduating from Lake Forest College, he earned his Master of Divinity from Princeton University, and Master of Ministry from Seattle Pacific University. A popular author whose books have sold several million copies, he recently gave this message at The Crystal Cathedral.*

# No Safe Place

## Bruce Larson

L ast spring, my wife and I were thrilled to watch a marvelous saga unfold right outside our kitchen window. Not ten feet from our window is a beam that holds up a second floor porch. And two wrens came along and built a nest there. Straw by straw and twig by twig, they built this nest on this secure beam, under our porch, out of the sun, out of the rain, out of the wind. No marauding cats could get to them.

These two birds were lovers, and in time they had eggs and they sat on the eggs and the eggs hatched and three little birds emerged. And watching them day by day, we were thrilled, until the Monday after the earthquake struck.

We looked out and noticed that the nest had been dislodged and had fallen to the ground. The three baby birds were dead. The parents had picked the safest place in the world, we thought, to build their nest and to raise their young, and it was all in vain.

The second book of the Bible, Exodus, is the story of God leading His people out of bondage and into freedom and purpose. And an important part of the message we find in the Exodus story is that there is no safe place.

There is no safe place in life. And if we expect one, we will be very, very disappointed. Life is shaped by our expectations. If you have false expectations about God, life doesn't make sense. Your expectations affect your health, your attitude, your whole spiritual life.

We had a family reunion last summer—our three kids and their spouses and our six grandchildren. I heard a wonderful true story from our daughter. It seems her husband's sister is a conservationist, and she and her husband and their five-year-old son were driving up the coast of Florida on vacation when they saw a sign that said Naturist Camp. They decided that a naturist camp was the same as a naturalist camp. They drove in. They parked their car. They walked toward the beach in this naturist camp and found it was actually a nudist camp.

The first thing they saw was a whole bunch of people stark naked riding bicycles along a bike path. The five-year-old stopped, stared in amazement, and said, "Look at that, Mom and Dad, they're not wearing safety helmets." Those were his expectations. If you ride a bicycle, you'd better be properly protected.

**What We Know About God**

Now, Exodus tells us what to expect in terms of God's nature. What do we know about God? We know from the Bible, beginning with Genesis and ending with Revelation, that God is our parent. God created us. God made us in His own image. And we know that God loves us. That is who God is, a parent who loves us, who delivers children from trouble. That's exactly what a parent does.

So Exodus tells us two very important things about God. First, that God is always with us. Second, that God has a purpose for us.

There are eight words that can change your life. I suggest
you say them every day and many times during the day.
The eight words are "I am never alone. I have a purpose."
In the best of times or worst of times, you can believe
that. However we feel, we are not alone and we have a
purpose. Those are eight words to build your life on.

Exodus is the wonderful story about God. But it is also
the story of God's people of purpose, the Israelites. And
it becomes our story as well.

They have moved to Egypt because of a famine in
Palestine. Jacob's son, Joseph, is already there and has
become the number two man in the court of the pharaoh.
To save their lives, they leave their land of drought and
famine to come to the green, lush valley of the Nile, where
the family grows and prospers. Generations go by, until
a new pharaoh comes to power who knows nothing about
Joseph and sees these people as a threat. He enslaves them.
The place of deliverance, the place of blessing, the place
of life becomes a place of slavery. God uses Moses to lead
His people out of there.

What do we make of all this? Three things: expect
blessings; let go of your blessings; and look beyond your
blessings for the meaning of life.

### Expect Blessings

Certainly, we can expect blessings. If God is our parent,
if God is ever present with us and He loves us, then He
will want to help us in our times of trouble.

If we, as imperfect parents, go to great lengths to deliver
our children, how much more will God do so. When my
children were young and still living under my roof, I often
had to rescue them. Love does that—and loses count of
the times.

I can remember trips to the principal's office to retrieve
a troublemaker. I can remember trips to the emergency

room at the hospital. I can remember trips to appease angry neighbors. I can remember trips to recover a banged-up car. I can remember trips to confront teachers who seemed to be persecuting my children. I can even remember a trip to the police station to pick up a wayward teenager. A loving parent delivers his or her children from the perils of life—whether they are in trouble they deserve and helped to create, or whether they are victims of an unfeeling and corrupt society. Love delivers, whenever possible.

If we, being earthly parents, are willing to do this, how much more does God want to deliver us from our problems?

If you believe that, you have great expectations. Martin Seligman, in his great book *Learned Optimism,* says all people have in their hearts one of two words—a yes or a no. A yes says, I am loved. I am special. There's a God who made me, I can trust Him. A no says, Things are bad and they're going to get worse.

My theology could be summed up in one sentence: Some people always find a parking place; some people never find a parking place. People with a yes in their hearts are part of the first group. They believe things will work out.

So expect blessings. If we, as parents know how to deliver and rescue and bless our kids, how much more will God? Expect it. Build your life around that belief.

### Let Go of Your Blessings

But secondly, we may need to let go of those blessings. If we hang on to them, they can become a place of slavery. The very thing God gave you is not meant to become a forever safe place. There is no safe place. Our blessings can turn into traps as they did for the Israelites.

Let's say, for example, you're single. You may be praying, "Oh, Lord, I'm so lonely. Send me a spouse—a husband, a wife." God hears those prayers and you meet somebody and you marry.

But the person you marry is somebody just like you, imperfect and flawed. He or she cannot be the answer to your life, however wonderful your spouse is. And so you become disappointed and disgruntled and feel there must be more than this. There is no more than this— marriage, alone, does not bring total fulfillment.

Perhaps, you've prayed for a family, for children. You have some and eventually one of two things happen. Either they disappoint you or they grow up and leave home. You can't build your life around your kids, as wonderful as they are.

Or you may have prayed for a job and gotten one, but that may not be a safe place. A new pharaoh may come along who knew not Joseph. A new boss may come along who did not hire you, who doesn't know the eighty-hour weeks you put in, who doesn't know how you rescued the company, who doesn't know the brilliance you've displayed in the past. The new management comes in and says, "I've never heard of her." Your unrewarding job becomes a place of stress and tension. If you've built your life around your job, that rarely is a safe place.

A friend of mine is an eagle watcher. And every summer he goes to British Columbia to observe eagles and to take notes on their habits. The largest eagle in the valley he had nicknamed Boss. One day, Boss was grabbing the thermals and soaring around, when he suddenly plummeted down to the valley, grabbed some prey and flew away with it in his talons. So my friend watched through his binoculars. He saw this big eagle begin to weave and fly erratically and then stumble and crash into a cliff, dropping like a stone to the canyon floor. My friend decided to climb down to the bottom of the canyon to see if he could find him. Some time later, he came upon the eagle and discovered he had caught a badger in his claws.

A badger, you know, is a mean animal. As Boss was flying away with his prize, the badger was eating out his stomach. Had the eagle let go of his prize, he would have lived. And there's a message here. God may deliver you from poverty, from loneliness, from childlessness, or meaninglessness, but don't count on that being a permanently safe place.

## Look Beyond Your Blessings

I urge you, instead, to look beyond your blessings because God has a purpose for you. God has a purpose for your life beyond making you comfortable and giving you blessings. God wants to make us partners to bring His love and His caring to people around us.

At last summer's reunion, I watched my three children and their spouses take care of their children. They seemed to be hovering over them a good deal of the time. How are you, darling? Do you want some more lunch? Are you getting sunburned? Do you need a nap? They are concerned for the comfort of their children, which at ages two to eight is understandable.

But picture those same parents with their children twenty years from now. If their primary concern is to make their children comfortable, they're failing as parents.

We have different concerns for our twenty-five or thirty-year-old child. The purpose of life is to find out the purpose of life. We want to know what they are doing with their lives. There's more to life than being comfortable. God has promised to take care of us, but we are also called to enter into the adventure and the romance of life, which is to be a part of God's purpose in the world.

The meaning of life is not security but significance. The meaning of life is not abundance, as good as that is, but significance. The meaning of life is not even good health. The point is what do we do with our good health or our wealth or our position or our status or our power or our comfortableness. God, as our parent, wants to make us comfortable, but we must not stop there. If we do, the earthquake may come and shake us off that safe perch.

Helen Keller understood that. This blind and deaf luminous saint said security doesn't exist. Animals never know it and children seldom do. Life is either an adventure or it is nothing.

I received a letter recently from one of the members of the Crystal Cathedral, where I serve. Here's what she wrote: "Harry and I live near Pioneer Park on Chapman Avenue. I was going by there one morning and God said, 'There Darlene, that's the place!' The following Saturday, I went to the store, bought two dozen eggs, one pound of bacon, bread, and bananas. I went home, fixed a pot of coffee, cooked breakfast, and took my picnic basket to the park. There, I spread out the tablecloth and the breakfast. One person was there and all I said was, 'Would you like to share my breakfast?' He stated that there were two other fellows asleep over in the bushes and could they come and eat too? 'Of course,' I said. I was thrilled.

"Anyway, the group on Saturday grew to sometimes twenty-five or thirty. Every Saturday I would ask when I went to the store, 'How much should I buy, Lord?' I always bought the right amount.

"The first thing I would do when I arrived at the park would be to give everyone a big hug. We would then join hands and have prayer. I would not preach to them. I would just let them know that I love them and then let them ask whatever they wanted to know about anything.

"These poor children of God—alcoholics, drug users, prostitutes, mothers with small children—I loved them all and they knew it. They told me many times they didn't care if I didn't bring food. They just wanted me to come and talk to them."

Darlene is somebody who has gone beyond looking for a safe place in life, to saying, "God, how can I be part of your purpose to bless people?"

God does want to bless you. Believe that. Become an optimist. But God wants more for you and me than deliverance from our problems. God wants to make us full partners in blessing others and building the kingdom. Don't settle for deliverance. Build your life on the Deliverer. Build your life, not on the answers to your problems, but on the one who gives the answers.

One of my favorite poems is called "The Marshes of Glen." The last line is, "As the marsh hen builds a nest on the watery sod, so I will build my life on the greatness of God."

Remember those words that can change your life. "I am never alone. I have a purpose."

*Dorothy Cross wanted to be a teacher from the time she was a child in Little Rock, Arkansas. A doctor of ministry now, she is Pastor of Spiritual Formation at the Hollywood Presbyterian Church, and a much-sought-after speaker on renewal.*

# How Prayer Helps You Cope and Win

## Dorothy Cross

These are stressful times. Everything seems to be falling apart. There doesn't appear to be any hope for the world, much less for us as individuals. However, there is *Good News*. And the good news is that there is Good News. It is because of that Good News (The Gospel of Christ) that we are called to come together in the Spirit of Love; give praise to God; and pray for both the world and ourselves.

Ageless saying that it is, "Prayer changes things," it really does. But you say to yourself, "Yes, I've heard that phrase quoted many times, but I'm afraid the problems I have are beyond changing." Then you ask, "What kind of prayer should I pray? How can I pray in a way that will make God want to listen to me?"

All the secrets of effective prayer are in the Bible. The best example of it is found in the 6th Chapter of the Gospel of Matthew. It is *The Lord's Prayer,* the one prayer you can count on to bring you the right answer. We forget it was the prayer that Jesus, Himself, gave His disciples after they asked Him to teach them how to pray.

## Four Powerful Words

The key to success with prayer lies in four words, "Thy will be done." They are the second request made in The Lord's Prayer. You know how it reads. After addressing God as our Father and honoring His name, comes, "Thy Kingdom come . . ."—and next in line are those famous words, "Thy will be done. . . ."

However, Jesus didn't intend us to pray those words with resignation, as if whatever will be will be. That's the attitude-trap we humans are all prone to get caught in. "Thy will be done" was only part of the point He was making. He really meant, "Thy will be done *on earth as it is in Heaven.*" That puts a whole different light on what He actually said. Jesus was teaching that we should not only pray for His Kingdom to come to earth, but also that His will would be done perfectly on earth, just as it is done in Heaven. Now since Heaven is a *perfect* place, why wouldn't we want to say, "Thy will be done on earth as it is in Heaven," and all in one breath? Have you ever noticed how in church unison prayer, the congregation always stops for a breath before they continue with that sentence? And, even though they may not mean it that way, the tone is always one of resignation.

God wants us to pray with faith and a forward-look, knowing that in His own good time, He will work out a perfect answer to our prayer. Sometimes the answer will be instantaneous; sometimes it will be *eventually,* and sometimes it will be a "No." We just have to accept in faith that "God moves in mysterious ways His wonders to perform." Remember how the old hymn goes? Below are its reassuring words. I suggest you memorize the third stanza.

God moves in a mysterious way His wonders to perform;
He plants His footsteps in the sea, and rides upon the
    storm.
Deep in unfathomable mines of never-failing skill
He treasures up His bright designs, and works His sovereign
    will.
Ye fearful saints, fresh courage take; the clouds ye so much
    dread
Are big with mercy, and shall break in blessings on your
    head.
Blind unbelief is sure to err, and scan His work in vain;
God is His own Interpreter, and He will make it plain.

William Cowper, 1774

**Our Father Knows Best**

When we are willing to whole-heartedly pray, "Thy will
be done here on earth as it is in Heaven," and ask Him
to do what He knows is best for us, that's when things
will begin to change. Many of us overlook that opportunity,
because we are afraid to seek His will—afraid He will want
us to do something we don't want to do. Sometimes it is
a rebellious spirit that wants to take over, when we think
we know more than God does about what would be best
for us. That isn't too surprising, because we are all self-
willed by nature. In a way, we are caught in a paradox.
In this world, we are required to exercise will power to
get things done, yet be willing to relinquish our will to
God's will at the same time.

**The Rewards of Seeking His Will**

But it is in seeking God's will that He is able to provide
more love, more purity, more power, and more joy in our
everyday lives. Even when we're waiting for those "eventual"

answers to our "Thy will be done" prayers, we can praise and thank Him for what he has done for us already.

As we cope with life, we must remember that God's will is what brings more good into our lives and affairs. As we cope with health problems, we need to remember that God's will for us is abundant joyous health. The Old Testament reminds us frequently that His will for us is good health. The New Testament continues that affirmation. Jesus' time on earth was spent teaching, healing, cleansing, casting out demons, and raising the dead. He was always concerned about hurting people.

## When Stress Closes In

When the intense moments of stress are about to overtake us, think first of God and your "Thy will be done" prayer. His will for us is peace of mind and completeness. You may be looking only at the stress of the moment, while God is seeing the whole picture and knows what the best answer would be. The stress will fade away. That simple prayer, when uttered in honest simplicity, will cover every situation. Of course, He wants us to tell Him our troubles and make our requests known, but to trust Him for the right solution.

In this topsy-turvy world, we know that sometimes we will win and sometimes we will lose. However, if we honestly try to keep our lives in tune with His perfect will, we'll win more often than we lose. Above all, try not to let doubt or pride get in the way. Seasoned Christians have found that it is far better to seek and trust His will than to resist it. If you are tempted to doubt God's intentions, remember that His will for you is your highest good. He is always ready to bring something good into your life. Keep yourself tuned to look for His highest and His best, and you'll soon see some encouraging surprises coming your way. Watch for them, though, or they might pass you by.

Keep praising God for who He is and where you are right now. Praise is based on total acceptance of the present moment as part of His loving, perfect will for you.

### Love: Another Way to Cope—and Win

Love is another crucial part of the solution to coping with life's problems and daily struggles. The more love we give, the more we will receive. We are reminded in Scripture to "Cast your bread upon the water. . . ." So cast your bread of love upon the waters of life, and in the days ahead, it will return to you, sometimes in ripples and sometimes in waves. But like the law of the echo, you have to be the originator of the love that comes to you. An echo is an amazing thing, isn't it. It sends back exactly what you send out. So don't ever send hate. Send love. The love you send begins in your heart. Keep asking God in prayer to send you a new supply of love for each day. He has promised to give us all we can take.

One of the first Bible verses a young child learns in Sunday School is, "Love one another." It is that give-and-take-of-love for one another that adds luster to life, and helps us maintain a winning spirit.

### Let Your Prayers Be Joyous

So let your "Thy will be done" prayers consist of joyous and effortless thanksgiving to God for His wondrous works. Meditate on His allness and His perfection. See Him in all things and give thanks for His presence there. Look at every situation as a perfect demonstration of the Father's wisdom and love for you. Bless everything and everybody as you bless the Father, Himself. Do all these things with patience and faith, and all will be made clear to you. God will reveal Himself to you in all His glory. He will give you, through your own recognition of His power, the desires of your heart. Remember "It is the Father's good pleasure to give you the kingdom."

And always, when you pray those four famous words, "Thy will be done," be sure that without hesitation you add, "on earth as it is in Heaven." Thank and praise Him for His wisdom and love, and look forward to each new day with faith, gratitude and hope. That's how prayer can help you cope successfully with life—and win.

*Born in Montpelier, Vermont, Dr. Terry Fullam attended the Eastman School of Music, graduated from Gordon College, and did post-graduate work at Boston University and Harvard. In 1967, he was ordained to the Episcopal priesthood, in the early '70's, becoming rector of St. Paul's Episcopal Church in Darien, Connecticut. For 17 years, he and his congregation developed an acclaimed renewal-ministry to help churches come alive—an adventure to which he now devotes full time.*

# The Prayer God Can't Resist

## Everett L. Fullam

St. Paul tells us twice in the New Testament that the things that happen to the people of the Old Testament were written down for our sake so we could learn from their experience. Today I want to look at a strange experience that King Solomon had, an experience which can teach us a lot about prayer and the will of God.

The account is found in I Kings, the 3rd chapter. Here we are introduced to Solomon who has just been declared the new king. He is king by the will of God—he understands that—and also by the will of his father. He comes to this post having been prepared for it. He believes that God is behind this move and he comes with a strong sense of divine calling. He is a person who is convinced that he is serving God in what he is doing and that he has been called by God to do it.

The account that I am concerned with takes place shortly after his inauguration as the new king. He has a dream.

In the middle of the night, God comes to him and says something very strange. The Lord says, "Solomon, you can ask me for anything you want and I will do it."

Think about that for a moment. "You can ask for anything you want and I will do that." Sounds to me like a blank check. It sounds to me as though God is saying, "You just fill in anything you want and I will do it." I wonder what you would answer. What would you put in that place if you knew that God would do whatever it was you wanted Him to do? What would you put in there?

I suppose a lot of people might ask for a lot of money. They would want success; they would want prosperity. Maybe others, a bit more wise, might ask for good health and a long life. Isn't it perfectly clear to you that anybody who had such a chance—to have one thing they could ask of God and be guaranteed that He would do—would certainly not fritter this away on something that is casual and of no consequence? Isn't it clear to you that such a person would want to think carefully about it, wouldn't want to waste this opportunity? Isn't it also clear to you that whatever they finally decided to ask of God would be a kind of x-ray of the soul? It would let you know a lot about what is important to them.

This blank check that God seems to have given to Solomon, "Ask anything you want from me and I'll give it to you," is found elsewhere in the scripture. Jesus is recorded in Mark 11:24 as saying much the same thing. "Anything you ask, if you believe that you will receive it, you will have it."

Again it seems as though it is a blank check and the only contingency is that you believe that you will receive it. You know as well as I that people can talk themselves into believing anything.

I remember a charming little scene in *Mill on the Floss.* Maggie Tulliver is about to take an examination for which she is ill prepared. Somehow she remembers that passage of scripture from the sermon of the week before in her local parish. She says, "Well, I am going to try it out. I am going to pray, 'Lord, help me to pass this examination and get a good grade.' " She flunks. She says that from then on she has given up on prayer. It doesn't work.

Well, that is not the only place that one finds Jesus making this kind of blank check statement.

John 14:13-14 says much the same thing. He says, "Anything you ask, asking in my name, I will give you."

What could be clearer? There are people who have built a whole doctrine of prayer on that one verse, but there is a problem with that. There are countless numbers of people who have tried that and they have found that it has not worked for them all the time.

You see, prayer is not really a matter of formula. It is not a matter of just trying something out, just saying what you want God to do and then expecting Him to do it. It doesn't work that way. You can't base a doctrine of prayer on any one verse of the scripture. You need to take all that it says and put it together and you find that some of these things are corrected and balanced out.

I'm thinking of what John says in I John 5. He makes this statement, "This is the confidence we have in the Lord; that if we ask anything according to His will, we know that He hears us. And if we know that he hears us, we know that we have the answer that we required of Him."

The contingency there is asking according to the will of God. I want to think more about that in terms of this experience with Solomon. Solomon's response is not immediately to answer the Lord with his request. Instead he begins to think about his godly heritage. Solomon answered, "You have shown great kindness to your servant, my father David, because he was faithful to you and righteous and upright in heart."

He remembered his father, a man with tremendous failings as well as great faith. Impossible that Solomon could have reached adulthood without understanding that his father in a moment of terrible lapse was responsible for adultery and murder. When it was pointed out to David what he had done, in repentance he confessed it to the whole world. Everyone knew what he had done, but he was a man of God and you can see the impact he had on his son.

Solomon showed his love for the Lord by walking according to the statutes of his father, David. He showed his love for the Lord by following in the footsteps and the counsel of his father. He not only had his example; he did have his counsel.

We read this in the chapter before: "When the time drew near for David to die, he gave a charge to Solomon his son. 'I am about to go the way of all the earth,' he said. 'So be strong, Solomon, show yourself a man, and observe what the Lord your God requires: Walk in His ways, keep His decrees and commands, His laws and requirements, as written in the Law of Moses, so that you may prosper in all you do and wherever you go.' "

Solomon had the godly example of his father and his counsel as well. What did he answer? Remember the word of God to him? "Solomon, ask for whatever you want and I will do it." He says, "Now, O Lord my God, you have made your servant king in place of my father David. But I am only a little child and I do not know how to carry out my duties."

Isn't that extraordinary? Solomon was not a little child. Solomon was a grown man. Solomon had emerged not as the eldest son, but had emerged as his father's successor. He now was on the throne. But you see, in his own eyes he was a humble man. He said, "I am just as a child. I don't know how to do what you are asking me to do."

Then comes his request of the Lord. Listen to it. "Lord, give your servant a discerning heart to govern your people and to distinguish between right and wrong. For who is able to govern this great people of yours?"

What was it Solomon asked for? He could have had anything or so it seemed. What he actually asked for was the ability to accomplish what God had assigned for him to do. That is a prayer I believe that is irresistible to God. He asked nothing for himself.

What he asked for was the ability to discern, to be a leader who could see into the nature of the things going on around him, who could understand what was happening and know the course of action that was to be taken. He asked for the ability to distinguish between that which is good and that which is evil. I wonder if it was as confusing in his day as it seems to be in ours. He wanted the clear ability to discern good from evil so that he might govern the people of the Lord justly.

You see, the prayer that is irresistible to God is whenever we ask Him for the grace, the strength, the wisdom, the insight, the knowledge, the courage, the resources to accomplish what he has assigned us to do. That is a prayer irresistible to God.

Now listen to the Lord's response: "The Lord was pleased that Solomon had asked for this. So God said to him, 'Since you have asked for this and not for long life or wealth for yourself, nor have you asked for the death of your enemies but for discernment in administering justice, I will do what you have asked. Solomon, I am going to give you the wisdom you need. I am going to give you the discerning mind; I am going to give you the moral sense to distinguish between that which is right and that which is wrong, that which is true, that which is false, that which is good and that which is evil. I am going to do it for you.' "

Then, a little bonus. Listen to this: "I will give you a wise and discerning heart but I will also give you what you have not asked for—both riches and honor—so that in your lifetime you will have no equal among kings. And if you walk in my ways and obey my statutes and commands, as David your father did, I will give you a long life."

What kind of prayer is it that God finds irresistible? Prayer in harmony with His will. I have to say to you that we don't have to know the will of God in order to choose it. We don't have to understand all things in order to embrace God's purpose for our lives. Our ignorance does not stop His hand, but our willfulness does.

We can choose God's purpose for us this day and tomorrow and the day after. We can say, "Lord, lead us into the good works that You have prepared for us to walk in. Give us discerning minds; give us the ability to distinguish that which is good and that which is bad; give us the power that we do what You want us to do by the grace that You supply." That, I believe, is a prayer irresistible to God. He gave an answer affirmative to Solomon and I believe it will be exactly the same for you and for me.

*Father, seal to our hearts this truth, simple as it is and let it challenge us, feed us, correct us, encourage us that in all things You may be glorified through that which we pray, that which we do. In the name of Jesus. Amen.*

*Catherine Marshall LeSourd, one of the most beloved and best-selling authors of this age, was born in Johnson City, Tennessee. In college, she met and later married Peter Marshall, who became the pastor of the prestigious New York Avenue Presbyterian Church in Washington, D.C. and Chaplain of the United States Senate. He died suddenly of a heart attack at 46, and Catherine's first book,* A Man Called Peter *was about him.*

*Later she met Leonard LeSourd to whom she was married for 23 years, until in 1983 she left this earth to be with the One she had so faithfully served and written about.*

# Let God Take Charge
## Catherine Marshall LeSourd

After the discovery that faith in God can make life an adventure, comes the desire to experiment with prayer. Like most people, I was full of questions, such as why are some agonizingly sincere prayers granted while others are not?

Many years later I still have questions. Mysteries about prayer are always out ahead of present knowledge—luring, beckoning on to further experimentation.

But one thing I do know; I learned it through hard experience. It is a way of prayer that has consistently resulted in a glorious answer, glorious because each time power beyond human reckoning has been released. This is the Prayer of Relinquishment.

I got my first glimpse of it in the fall of 1943. Tuberculosis had kept me in bed for many months. A bevy of specialists seemed unable to help. Persistent prayer, using all the faith I could muster, had resulted in—nothing.

One afternoon a pamphlet was put in my hand. It was the story of a missionary who had been an invalid for eight years. Constantly she had prayed that God would make her well, so that she might do His work. Finally, worn out with futile petition, she prayed, "All right. I give up. If You want me to be an invalid for the rest of my days, that's Your business. Anyway, I've discovered that I want You even more than I want health. You decide." The pamphlet said that within two weeks the woman was out of bed, completely well.

This made no sense to me. It seemed too pat. Yet I could not forget the story. On the morning of September fourteenth (how can I ever forget the date?) I came to the same point of abject acceptance. "I'm tired of asking" was the burden of my prayer. "I'm beaten, finished. God, You decide what you want for me for the rest of my life. . . ." Tears flowed. I had no faith as I understood faith. I expected nothing. The gift of my sick self was made with no trace of graciousness.

The result was as if windows had opened in heaven; as if some dynamo of heavenly power had begun flowing, flowing into me. From that moment my recovery began.

### God Was Teaching Me Something About Prayer

God was trying to teach me something important about prayer. Still I got only part of the message. I saw that the demanding spirit—"God, I must have thus and so: God, this is what I want you to do for me—" is not real prayer and hence receives no answer. I understood that the reason for this is that God absolutely refuses to violate our free will and that therefore, unless self-will is voluntarily given up, even God cannot move to answer prayer. But it was going to take more time and more experience for me to begin to understand the Prayer of Relinquishment.

Part of that understanding has come through learning of other people's experiences with this type of prayer. It has been exciting to uncover in contemporary life, in the

Bible, and scattered through the writings of men in other centuries the infallible power of this prayer technique.

Some years ago, I stumbled across one example in the life of a New England writer, Nathaniel Hawthorne. In 1853 Hawthorne had decided to take his family abroad for an extended stay. He wanted a broadening of his horizons, contact with other writers in England and Italy. By then he was already recognized as a master of the craft of the short story through his "Twice-Told Tales," and was famous as the author of the successful novel, *The Scarlet Letter.*

In late 1858, the Hawthornes were settled in a villa in Rome. February 1860 found them in the midst of a grave crisis. Una, their eldest daughter, was dying of a virulent form of malaria. The attending physician, Dr. Franco, had that afternoon warned the distraught parents that unless the young girl's fever abated before morning she would die.

As Sophia Hawthorne sat by her daughter's bed, her thoughts went to her handsome husband in the adjoining room. She could picture him—his troubled blue eyes, that splendid head with its mop of dark hair, bowed in grief. She recalled what he had said earlier that day. "I cannot endure the alternations of hope and fear, and therefore I have settled with myself not to hope at all."

But Sophia could not share Nathaniel's hopelessness. Una could not, must not die. This daughter strongly resembled her father, had the finest mind, the most complex character of all the Hawthorne children. Why should a capricious Providence demand that they give her up?

Moreover, Una had been delirious for several days and had recognized no one. Were she to die this night, there would not even be the solace of farewells.

As the night deepened, the young girl ceased her incoherent mutterings and lay so still that she seemed to be in the anteroom of death. The mother went to the window and looked out on the piazza. There was no moonlight; heavy clouds scudded across a dark and silent sky.

"I cannot bear this loss—cannot—cannot." Then, suddenly, unaccountable, another thought took over. "Why should I doubt the goodness of God? Let Him take Una, if He sees best. I can give her to Him. No, I won't fight against Him any more."

Then an even stranger thing happened. Having made the great sacrifice in her mind, Sophia expected to feel sadder. Instead she felt lighter, happier than at any time since Una's long illness had begun.

Some minutes later she walked back to the girl's bedside and felt her daughter's forehead. It was moist and cool. The pulse was slow and regular. Una was sleeping naturally. Sophia rushed into the next room to tell her husband that the crisis seemed to be past. She was right. Though Una was months getting the malaria out of her system, she did recover completely.

**The Intriguing Question**

The intriguing question is: What is the spiritual law implicit in this Prayer of Relinquishment? I think I know at least part of it. . . We know that fear blocks prayer. Fear is a barrier erected between us and God, so that His power cannot get through us. So—how does one get rid of fear?

This is not easy when the life of someone dear hangs in the balance, or when what we want most in all the world seems to be slipping away. At such times, every emotion, every passion, is tied up in the dread that what we fear most is about to come upon us. Obviously only strong measures can deal with such a powerful fear. My experience has been that trying to overcome it by turning one's thoughts to the positive or by repeating affirmations is not potent enough.

It is then that we are squarely up against the law of relinquishment. Was Jesus showing us how to use this law when He said, "resist not evil?" In God's eyes, fear is evil because it is acting out of lack of trust in Him. So Jesus is advising, "Resist not fear."

In other words, Jesus is saying: "Admit the possibility of what you fear most. And lo, as you stop fleeing, as you force yourself to walk up to the fear, as you look it full in the face never forgetting that God and His power are still the supreme reality, the fear evaporates." Drastic? Yes. But effective.

One point about the Prayer of Relinquishment puzzled me for many years. There seemed to be a contradiction between the Prayer of Faith and that of relinquishment. If relinquishment is real, the one praying must be willing to receive or not receive this heart's desire. But that state of mind scarcely seems to exhibit the faith that knows that one's request will be granted. and as I read the gospels, Jesus placed far greater stress on the Prayer of Faith than on the Prayer of Relinquishment.

Now I believe I have the explanation. The fact is that I went through a period of misunderstanding faith. Once I thought that faith was believing this or that specific thing in my mind with never a doubt. Now I know that faith is nothing more or less than *actively trusting God.*

### A Peter Marshall Story About "Active Trust"

Peter Marshall liked to illustrate what such active trust means by a homely example:

> Suppose a child has a broken toy. He brings the toy to his father, saying that he himself has tried to fix it and has failed. He asks his father to do it for him. The father gladly agrees . . . takes the toy . . . and begins to work. Now obviously the father can do

his work most quickly and easily if the child makes no attempt to interfere, simply sits quietly watching, or even goes about other business, with never a doubt that the toy is being successfully mended. But what do most of God's children do in such a situation? Often we stand by offering a lot of meaningless advice and some rather silly criticism. We even get impatient and try to help, and so get our hands in the Father's way, generally hindering the work. . . . Finally, in our desperation, we may even grab the toy out of the Father's hands entirely, saying rather bitterly that we hadn't really thought He could fix it anyway. . . that we'd given Him a chance and He had failed us.

Grabbing the toy away is certainly not trust. But what does demonstrate trust is to put the thing or the person one loves best into the Father's hands to do with as he sees fit. Thus faith is by no means absent in the Prayer of Relinquishment. In fact this prayer is faith-in-action.

And that is why this prayer is answered, even when the one making the relinquishment has little hope that what he fears most can be avoided. For I have always felt that God is not half so concerned with what we do. It's the act of placing what we cherish most in His hands that is to Him the sweet music of the essence of faith.

**Out of My Own Experience**

My own latest adventure with the Prayer of Relinquishment came in connection with the mundane problem of household help. In the weeks prior to my marriage to Leonard LeSourd, I was happily excited but at the same time panicky at the thought of taking on three young children. After all, I had thought myself finished with child-rearing. Peter John had then been out of the home nest for three years, away at school. At the same time I wanted to keep on with my writing. What if I was not adequate to the situation?

In his efforts to reassure me, Len made solemn promises of household help. But after our marriage, the help was slow in materializing. Three months passed, four. One maid stayed for three weeks, then decided to go back to her home in North Carolina. Then a cleaning woman who was helping me one day a week had to stop when she fell and injured her leg.

Many a morning Len and I prayed about it. Soon after our marriage, we had hit upon a pleasant way to begin our day with quietness and prayer. An automatic coffee pot attached to a clock would waken us with the fragrance of percolating coffee. Then we would sit propped up in bed, sipping coffee, reading a portion of Scripture together, thinking through the day ahead.

One morning I was particularly discouraged. I was caught between all my blessings—a wonderful husband, three lovely children at home and a fourth in and out, a big new house, and my daily writing. I was, quite frankly, exhausted. We had tried everything we knew: agencies, the suggestions of friends and relatives, the "Help Wanted" columns in the local and New York newspapers. Just the evening before a promising candidate from Boston with whom we had been corresponding had telephoned that she could not come.

### Lord, We've Tried Everything

So once more we took the situation to God. . . . "Lord, we've tried everything we can think of. Every road has seemed a dead end. Doors have been so consistently shut in our faces that You must be trying to teach us something. Tell us what it is—"

There followed the illumination that prayer often brings. In this case, it was not pleasant. I had been trying to dictate the terms of my life to God—what I wanted: help in the home so that I could get on with my writing. A thought stabbed me. What if—for this period of my life—I was supposed to give up the writing? Immediately this possibility brought tears. Why should I have to relinquish something which I had from the beginning dedicated to God—and something from which I also got such satisfaction? Still it was obvious that our home and the children had to come first. So, knowing that I would get no answer from God until I was willing to surrender the writing, I set myself to the task.

### The Principle of "The Will"

Resolutely I set my will to accept what had to be accepted. Though my emotions were in stark rebellion, I knew that sooner or later they would fall into line. I plunged into homemaking, completing the furnishing and decorating of the house . . . meals . . . laundry . . . groceries . . . creating an atmosphere of security for children who badly needed it.

Then I realized that, beyond the writing, there had been another reason why I had wanted help. It was the haunting fear that I would be physically and emotionally unable to handle all the housework, take care of the children, be a good wife to my husband—all at one time. But now I was learning that I could cope with it. With that knowledge came the self-assurance that washed away all fears. And I would never have had this sense of security and confidence if we had started our marriage with domestic help.

When the relinquishment was complete, the break-through occurred. Unexpected a letter came from Boston. The woman who had refused us before said that she was now available. Lucy Arsenault came to us. Lucy—settled, reliable, a superb cook, a rare person. As always, a loving God had planned so much better than we ever could have.

### Resignation is Barren of Faith

There is a difference between acceptance and resignation. One is positive; the other negative. Acceptance is creative—resignation is sterile.

Resignation is barren of faith in the love of God. It says: "Grievous circumstances have come to me. There is no escaping them. I am only one creature, an alien in a vast unknowable creation. I have no heart left even to rebel. So I'll just resign myself to what apparently is the will of God; I'll even try to make a virtue out of patient submission." So resignation lies down quietly in the dust of a universe from which God seems to have fled, and the door of Hope swings shut.

But turn the coin over. Acceptance says, "I trust the good will, the love of my God. I'll open my arms and understanding to what He has allowed to come to me. Since I know that He means to make all things work together for good, I consent to the present situation with hope for what the future will bring." Thus acceptance leaves the door of Hope wide open to God's creative plan. This difference between acceptance and resignation is the key to an understanding of the Prayer of Relinquishment. . . .

### Jesus' Example of A Surrendered Will

To the disciples of Jesus Christ, His actions during the last week of His life on earth must have seemed equally nonsensical. Their Master had a great following among common people. His disciples were hoping that he would use this following to overthrow the Roman grip on their little country and move, at last to establish His earthly kingdom.

Instead He deliberately set His feet on the path that would lead inescapably to the cross. He did not have to go up to Jerusalem that last time. He could have compromised with the priests, bargained with Caiaphas. The disciples were probably right in thinking that He could have capitalized on His following, appeased Judas, and set up the beginning of an earthly empire. Later Pilate would all but beg Him to say the right words so that he might release Him. Even in the Garden of Gethsemane on the night of betrayal, Christ had plenty of time and opportunity to flee.

But He would not flee. Instead He knelt to pray in the shadowy Garden under the gray-green leaves of the olive trees. And in His prayer that night, Jesus gave us, for all time, the perfect pattern for the *Prayer of Relinquishment.*

Jesus had been given genuine humanity, as well as divinity. Part of that humanity was His free will. He chose to use His free will to leave the decision to His Father as to whether He must die by execution.

Making that decision was such agony that as He knelt there He was not even aware of the beauty all around Him. The valley under the brow of the hill was washed in moonlight. Below Him the brook Kedron rippled and sang over stones and through rushes. Around Him were the myrtle trees, palms and fig trees that melted into the olive groves. And in the enclosed Garden of Gethsemane, all around Him were leaves and trunks of the olive trees silvered by filtering moonlight. This was not a world that Christ, the man, wanted to leave.

Was there a moment when He wondered how to pray about the terrible alternatives before Him? If so, in the end He knew only one prayer could release the power that was needed to lift a sin-ridden world: "My Father, if it is possible let me not have to drink this cup. Yet it is not what I want, but what you want" (Matthew 26:39, JBP).

In these words Jesus deliberately set Himself to make His will and God's will the same. The prayer was not answered as the human Jesus wished. Yet power has been flowing from His cross ever since.

God has given you and me free will too. And the voluntary giving up of our self-will always has a cross at the center of it. It is the hardest thing human beings are called on to do.

When we come right down to it, how can we make obedience real, except as we give over the self-will in all of life's episodes as they unfold? That is why it should not surprise us that at the center of answered prayer lies the *Law of Relinquishment.*

*Before becoming Chaplain of the United States Senate, Richard C. Halverson was senior pastor of the Fourth Presbyterian Church in Washington, D.C. He is the author of several books and has served on the boards of World Vision, USA, African Enterprise, and Concern Ministries, Inc.*

# Keep Your Faith in Focus

## Richard C. Halverson

In the first chapter of the book of Colossians, the Apostle Paul has one sentence that to me is life determining for each of us. The sentence is simply this, "All things were created by Christ, and for Christ." The prepositions are important.

"All things were created by Christ,"—He is the creator. ". . . and for Christ,"—He created all things for Himself. If words mean anything, it means that you and I who were created by Christ, were created for Christ, and we are never really ourselves until we belong to Christ, until He owns us and possesses us.

I am sure all of us have had the common experience of watching home moves, (for example 35mm slides) when the one who is projecting them gets the film out of focus. You know the nausea you almost feel sometimes and the element of confusion as he adjusts the projector back and forth and finally the relief that comes when the picture is back in focus. Our lives are very much that way. You know, the thing about focusing a picture is that when the central object is in focus, the whole field of vision is in focus in right relation to the central object. When the central object is out of focus, then the whole field of vision is out of focus and obscure.

## Out of Focus Drifters

I would like to suggest that there are two kinds of people whose lives are out of focus because they are not in focus on the central figure for whom they were created. There are those who are *drifters*. Their lives are aimless, their lives are purposeless, their lives are meaningless. They are like corks on waves, going in whatever direction the waves may be moving.

Some years ago I recall traveling across the desert with my family and we stopped at a restaurant at one of these intersections where you can see in all directions for many miles. The land is absolutely flat. While we were in the restaurant we watched a hitchhiker. At first he was standing along the road opposite from the restaurant and he was hitchhiking his way east. Car after car went past and no one picked him up. Finally, very reluctantly, he crossed the road and started thumbing his way west. And no car picked him up there. Then he turned the other way and started thumbing his way south. And finally he was thumbing his way north. That is the picture of so many of us. We are aimless in our lives, and our lives are out of focus because they are not in focus with the central figure of life—Jesus Christ.

## Those Who Are Driven Are Also Out of Focus

Then there is the other extreme—the person who is driven. This is the one who is obsessive, compulsive, machine-like in his operations. He has purpose, all right, but the purpose consumes him. Things begin to get out of focus because that which ought to be secondary becomes primary. He gets his values and goals wrong, and the ends become the means, and then everything is confused as this driven person forces his way through life following false gods, giving false priority to things that are really secondary and relatively unimportant in his life. His life, too, is out of focus with the central figure—the one he was intended to belong to, the one he was intended to serve. There is another kind of person, not the drifter, not the driven, but the one whose life has direction. He has purpose. Life has meaning. He is a directed person because he has discovered he was made for Jesus Christ, and he has given himself to Jesus Christ so that Christ not only owns him, having created him and having purchased him on the cross, but Christ possesses him because he has surrendered to the One he was made for.

### You Can Own What You Don't Possess— And Possess What You Don't Own

You can own what you don't possess, and you can possess what you don't own. I own some books which I do not possess because I have loaned them out to someone somewhere sometime ago, and I have forgotten and apparently they have forgotten. I don't complain, however, because strangely I have some books in my library I have borrowed from someone and forgotten from whom, so I possess them but I do not own them. My wife and I possess a home in Bethesda, Maryland, which is not ours. It belongs to the church. We call it a manse. But we live in it and for all practical purposes, it is ours.

So, you can own what you don't possess and you can possess what you don't own. Christ owns you and me. He owns us because He created us. he owns us because He paid the price of His own life on the cross for our eternal salvation. He owns us doubly. But He has created us with a free will—free moral agents. He has given us the option of allowing Him to possess us or allowing ourselves to be possessed by another. That is something we don't think about a great deal. If we are not owned and possessed by Jesus Christ, we can be possessed by the arch enemy of Jesus Christ—Satan, the devil. Oh, he doesn't let us know that. He is very wise and subtle. He is the master of masquerade. So he never allows us to think that we are possessed by him. He allows us to think that we are possessed, for example, by goals that drive us, possess us, and make us compulsive. He allows us to think that we are possessed by ourselves so we have aimless, drifting, purposeless, meaningless lives. We just think we are free, but actually we are just drifting. He is very wise in convincing us that he does not possess us because he knows that if we knew he did we would want to submit ourselves to Jesus Christ and be possessed by Him. So he hides the secret from us. The fact is that if you are not possessed by Jesus Christ, even though He owns you, you are possessed by Satan, however much he hides the secret from you.

If you were sensitive about your life, there would be many little clues in your lifetime to show that you are really controlled by the devil. You think you are your own master, but you are not and you know it. The times when you are all alone and you look at yourself, you realize that you are not your own. Then, if you are not your own, why not belong to the One who bought you for a price? That is what the Bible says, "You are not your own. You are bought with a price."

### You Can Be An Original—Or a Cheap Copy

Now that is your prerogative and mine. I love to visit the National Gallery of Art in Washington and spend time looking at the great masterpieces that hang on the walls painted by the artist himself on his own canvas with his own oils and brushes and strokes as he committed to canvas that which was in his soul. They are masterpieces and they are priceless because they are originals. But as you leave the National Gallery of Art, and just before you walk out on Constitution Avenue, there is a little shop in which you can buy a small copy of the original. It is just a photograph. It is beautiful but it is tiny. You can get it for about 50 cents. The original hangs on the walls of the Gallery. You can buy a cheap copy for 50 cents.

You and I have the option of being the divine original God intended, or just a cheap copy—a "might-have-been." Now that is entirely up to you and me. He owns us. He created us. And He created us for Himself. We were made to be His. We were made to be possessed by Him. We were made to be led by Him. We were made to be controlled by Him. Indeed we were made to be filled with Him! But He waits until we present our bodies as a living sacrifice. This is why the Apostle Paul made the point to the Corinthians, "Don't you know that your body is the temple of God, that the Holy Spirit of God dwells in you?" Don't you know what your bodies were made for? They were made for God. They were made for God to inhabit and He desires this. But He waits until we respond to His invitation, indeed to His exhortation.

### You and I Were Made By Christ For Christ

You and I were made *by* Christ *for* Christ. You and I can never be ourselves, never be what we ought to be until He possesses us. He does not possess us until we give ourselves to Him, until we respond to the exhortation in Romans 12:1-2. Some years ago I was speaking at a family conference in a camp called Mount Hermon, California. I had been there all weekend, and during that weekend

I met a very lovely lady. I was especially attracted to her. She was a beautiful woman and she was very gracious. To me she was 100% lady! I was very interested in her and we spent as many moments together as we could that weekend.

At the last meeting of the conference I spoke on the text Romans 12:1-2, "I beseech you therefore by the mercies of God that you present your bodies as a living sacrifice, holy and acceptable unto God, which is your reasonable service. Be not conformed to this world but be transformed by the renewing of your mind, that you may prove what is the good and acceptable and perfect will of God." When I finished the message, I told the story of Armin Gesswein, my Lutheran pastor friend, and then I said, "Now I want you folks to imagine that right under your chair there is an altar—right under your feet where you are sitting. If you would like to do what Paul, writing under the inspiration of the Holy Spirit, invites us to do, stand now on that altar." I had hardly gotten the invitation out and this woman was the first to stand, then an older man, and then many others. I wanted to find out why she stood so quickly because I had hardly given the invitation.

After the benediction, I got to her, and I said, "Do you mind if I ask why you were so quick to stand after the invitation?" This is what she said: "Dick, I am 88 years old. I have been a Presbyterian all my life. But tonight was the first time I knew that Christ wanted my body, and I didn't want to waste any time." Are you wasting time with whatever you are doing? Drifting? Driven? Or is your life directed by the God who made you for Himself?

You were made by Jesus Christ, and you will never be what you were created to be until you given yourself to Him. I want to invite you right now, wherever you are, to imagine that there is an altar under your feet. I invite you to heed the invitation and by standing on that altar, or just putting your feet on it as you remain seated, present yourself, your body, to Christ, and become His. Let Him possess you and control you. Then He will mold and fashion your life after the image of the divine original and you will be in no danger of being a cheap copy of what you might have been. Instead your faith will truly be "in focus."

*Now pastor of the Ogden Dunes Community Church in Portage, Indiana, Nancy Becker first entered the ministry as a Presbyterian pastor in Darien, Connecticut. A former English teacher, she is also a writer, with articles published in* The Christian Century, Leadership Journal, *and other periodicals.*

# Life is Like a Baseball Game

## Nancy Becker

Growing up in my father's house, it was not possible to be indifferent to the American League Pennant race. My father loved baseball. He was a Tiger fan, and he passed on the addiction to all of his children. From early spring until mid-October, it was part of the air we breathed. Whatever we were doing during the weekends, the voice of Van Patrick reporting the Tiger games was part of it.

And even now, when I hear the sounds of a baseball game on the radio, I still kind of "hearken to it." No matter who the teams are or what is happening in the game, there is something about the sound of baseball reporting that is different from anything else. Something about it just seems to get into one's blood. It's a world that intertwines with our daily life. Once you have spent a summer immersed in league standings and batting averages; once you have agonized through a tough pennant race with a team, you never quite recover from it.

The world of baseball is a dramatic presentation of some of life's most important and universal lessons. Now I'm not saying that Abner Doubleday intended to make a theological statement about the meaning of life when he invented the game of baseball. But he did invent a game which dramatizes a very human predicament—that of trying to measure up to a standard of perfection, and always falling short.

The Apostle Paul talked a lot about standards of perfection that are impossible to meet. To Paul, those standards were the Hebrew Law, set up to show us how inadequate we are. We can never be good enough because we cannot live up to its standards. "All have sinned and fallen short of the glory of God," he writes in his letter to the Roman Christians.

Well, baseball is a lot like that too. Baseball is a game of measuring things against impossible standards—a game of numbers. Everything is added up and written down *somewhere.* You can find the batting averages of all the players in the major leagues. You can read RBI's, and ERA's and fielding percentages—all lined up and compared to every other player in the league. A player's batting average is printed in the paper; it is announced over the radio and flashed in bright lights on the stadium scoreboard. All are carried out to the three decimal points. Nobody says, "He's hitting pretty well." They say, "He's hitting .276." Very precise measurements. This is no way to pretend success. There is no way to hide failure. It's all right there in the book.

And the interesting thing about it is that nobody does very well. The very best hitters get about three hits in every ten tries. That's not a very good percentage for most jobs, but if you get three out of ten in baseball, they give you a million dollar salary! And if you do it several years in a row, they put you in the Hall of Fame.

Take Mickey Mantle, for instance. Mantle was one of

the all-time greats of the game. He could hit towering home
runs from either side of the plate. Yet Mickey Mantle struck
out 1,710 times in his career. That's a lot of strike-outs.
And he is one of the all-time all-stars!

Nobody is very good when measured against the absolute
batting standard of 1,000. That's a tough standard to fall
short of—with the whole world watching. And everyone
falls short of it. No one has even come halfway to perfection
over the course of a season. All have fallen short. Paul
the Apostle would appreciate the similarities in the batting
average standard, and the inability of anyone to come
anywhere near living up to it. Baseball is a hard-judging
master of anyone who sets out to be good at it. And life
is a lot like that, too.

But there is another side of baseball. A side that is more
like the *gift of grace*. In baseball, everyone gets a chance
to bat. Everyone gets the same number of balls and strikes.
Each team gets the same number of outs. And what makes
baseball more fair than some other sports is that it has
no clock. And maybe this makes the game even more fair
than life itself. Because in baseball, you do not run out
of time. Unless it rains, both teams get their innings—as
many as it takes to decide who wins and who loses.

As that great baseball theologian, Yogi Berra, said, "It
ain't over til it's over." In baseball, there is always the
possibility that the unexpected will happen. There is always
time for redemption. Take the case of Bob Brenley, for
instance. Brenley is now helping Harry Carey broadcast
the Cubs games, but in 1986 he was playing third base
for the San Francisco Giants. In the fourth inning of the
game against the Atlanta Braves, Brenley made an error
on a routine ground ball. Four batters later, he kicked away
another grounder—and then, while he was scrambling to
recover, he threw wildly past home plate trying to get the
runner. Two errors on the same play! A few minutes later,
he muffed yet another play, to become the first player in

the 20th century to make four errors in one inning.

Those of us who have made very public errors in one situation or another can easily imagine how he felt during that long walk off the field at the end of that inning. But in the bottom of the fifth, Brenley hit a home run. In the seventh, he hit a bases-loaded-single, driving in two runs and tying the game. And then, in the bottom of the ninth, Brenley came up to bat again with two out. He ran the count to 3-to-2, after which he hit a massive home run into the left field seats to win the game for the Giants.

Brenley's scorecard for the day came to three hits in five at-bats, two home runs, four errors, four runs allowed, and four runs driven in, including the game-winning run.

Life is a lot like that—a mixture of hits and errors. And there is grace in that. Grace means you'll have another chance. Grace won't exactly erase your errors, but it will give you a chance to make up for them. If we are just .200 hitters, God will hit .800 to fill in the gaps. It's not over til it's over. There are still some surprises waiting. Paul puts it in his own words, "Since all have sinned and fallen short of the glory of God, they are justified by His grace as a gift, through the redemption which is in Jesus Christ . . . because in His divine forbearance He has passed over former sins."

Even the Apostle himself made a lot of errors in his own life. He was the Pharisee, the ultimate enemy of Jesus, the feared and hated persecutor of the early disciples, who had systematically attempted to destroy the church by annihilating its members. But Jesus found him and turned him around, and set him on a new course, building a church in which the forgiveness of Christ was offered to everyone— no membership tests, no lines of birth or race or accomplishment—a church for people who had made errors.

In fact, Jesus spent most of His time with people who had made a lot of errors. People who had gone 0 for 4 in life, so to speak; people who had often dropped the ball. "Losers" we might call them—uneducated fishermen, prostitutes, people afflicted with unpleasant diseases and mental disorders, tax collectors, the outcasts, the poor, the unacceptable, the lost. That's why He came—to seek and to save the lost.

In Christ, the scorekeeper cancels the errors. Gives the losers another chance, a new start, a new beginning. Jesus looks past the errors to the possibilities of the future. With God, it's not over til it's over. Nothing is finished until God is finished with it. No one is finished until God says so.

One of the chances we all get in life is the chance to make errors. All of us make mistakes, some more than others. But with Christ, we always have another chance. We always have the possibility of a comeback. God's love is always seeking us—always following us—always overlooking the errors and giving us still another inning—still another chance at bat.

'Cause it ain't over 'til it's over.

*In 1979, Joni Eareckson, a quadriplegic for 13 years, became the Founder and President of Joni and Friends, a non-profit organization which offers service and encouragement to the disabled. To this day she carries on her ministry with courage and compassion for others who have to cope daily with overwhelming lifetime handicaps.*

# My Wheelchair is My Classroom

## Joni Eareckson Tada

I knew something terrible had happened as I was being pulled from Chesapeake Bay that Sunday in late July, 1967. When I'd struck my head in a miscalculated dive and my whole body went numb, I realized that my swimming was over for the day. But I had no idea I would spend the rest of my life in a wheelchair.

I'd just graduated from high school and was looking forward to college and a career in sports. After lying helpless in a hospital bed for a year and a half after the accident, I was one bitter young woman even though I'd made a commitment to Christ in high school.

When I graduated to a wheelchair, I still couldn't see much purpose in my life. I hated being handicapped and didn't even want to be around other people who were in wheelchairs. It only underscored my own disability.

A lot of the handicapped people I knew were loud, nasty militants who chained themselves to inaccessible city halls—

or they were whining complainers who wanted others to feel sorry for them. I didn't want to have anything to do with them. But I kept sensing God speaking to my heart:

*Joni, I want you to touch the militants with My love. I want you to share My compassion with those who are filled with self-pity. What are you going to do about it?*

I didn't want to do anything about it. I argued, "God, You've got the wrong person. You need some sociologist who's gone through rehabilitation counseling to reach these people. Not me. Please don't call me into anything that's going to relate to disabled people, because I'm not like them."

The Lord wanted me to have His heart toward the disabled, to have Christ's compassion toward an individual who might drool, or smell bad, or sit in a wheelchair all twisted and gnarled. He loved such people and He wanted me to love them too.

It was only when I realized that Christ had laid down His life for them, as He had for me, that I could identify with these special people. Until then I'd been looking at the handicapped from a distance. I had to face the fact that I'm no different than the person with cerebral palsy. My need is the same as his: We both need Christ.

When I accepted the fact that I was one of the handicapped population, I began to experience God's love for the 42 million disabled people in America. What a difference that made the next time I went into a residential care facility for disabled people!

I realized that I was just like them. I knew then that there were people in the mainstream of life who would look at me and turn away. But God loves all of us.

Patiently, the Lord helped me accept myself as one of "them"—the disabled. Through the years the Lord has been my schoolmaster, and the wheelchair has been my classroom. With the help of God and the support of persistent therapists and praying friends and family, I have accomplished more than I ever dreamed I could.

I can type, write, and paint with my mouth. I have authored numerous articles and a dozen books, spoken before large audiences, and recorded song albums. I have been the subject of widely distributed films and videos. I head an international ministry called *Joni and Friends,* and I host a radio program that is carried on 600 stations. And all of this is done to share God's love and compassion.

People have told me, "You're so busy; your life is so complicated. You paint, you sing, your write, you talk, you do a radio program, you run a ministry, you're a wife." Yet the longer I live in a wheelchair, and the more I mature in Christ, the simpler my life becomes.

In spite of the many responsibilities the Lord has given me, life is incredibly simple. Whether it's through painting, writing, speaking, or being a good wife to my husband Ken, it all boils down to just loving Jesus and reflecting Him. I'm grateful that my wheelchair keeps forcing me to do that. . . .

In the dozen years we've been in the *Joni and Friends* ministry, I've been pleased at how far the Christian community has come in dealing with the disabled. Virtually all churches involved in building programs now include universal accessibility features—entrance ramps, wider hallways, washrooms equipped for people in wheelchairs. That's encouraging.

It's also encouraging to see that churches are becoming more involved in programs for the disabled. Christian education directors are initiating outreach to the handicapped and are turning to us for resources.

But there is still a long way to go. It's hard to change attitudes: People feel insecure around the disabled. Or they are just too preoccupied to get involved. Some harbor the misconception that a physical or mental disability is the result of individual sin. Sadly, the Christian population as a whole continues to walk a wide circle around the handicapped.

Before my own wheelchair education, I must confess I possessed a kindred attitude. Now, of course, I can identify with the handicapped. I've been privileged to meet impressive leaders who are doing a great work in evangelism, exhortation, or some other ministry. But I can't always relate to them.

The best model for correcting hurtful attitudes is Jesus Christ. He was constantly encountering people with disabilities. Of His 35 recorded miracles, 26 involved healing of handicapped people—the blind, the deaf, the paralyzed, the mentally ill. Jesus was not afraid to approach these people, which He did individually with care, compassion, and concern.

I believe it is significant that Jesus showed Himself as the Messiah through disabled people. When the disciples of John the Baptist came to Jesus and asked, "Are You the One who was to come?" He pointed to the fact that "the blind receive sight, the lame walk . . . the deaf hear" (Matt. 11:3-5, NIV).

Wouldn't it be marvelous if Christ chose to return in similar fashion? The Prophet Isaiah indicates that He might do just that: "He will come and save you. Then the eyes of the blind shall be opened, and the ears of the deaf shall be unstopped. Then shall the lame man leap as an hart, and the tongue of the dumb sing" (Isa. 35:4-6).

If Jesus is going to gather disabled people by His side on His return, then we should help get them prepared. We should work to get their hearts ready to receive Him as Lord so they can be a part of the victory celebration.

I want the disabled to know that Jesus, our suffering Servant, understands what they are going through. My own physical disablement has helped me better appreciate the suffering that Jesus experienced. When we get initiated into the fellowship of Christ's suffering, we get to know Him better.

There are many days when I don't have it "all together"

physically. I hate my handicap, I just want to go to be with Jesus, get my new glorified body, and have the pain wiped away.

It touches my heart when I see a small child with some severe disability and realize that he must go through years of frustration and heartache, Society, for the most part, will neglect him.I want Jesus to come soon and close the curtain on that kind of suffering.

I want the *Joni and Friends* ministry to always have God's redemptive plan as its focus. We must meet practical needs for the disabled, certainly, but the most important needs people have is to know Christ. My prayer is that we will always be available for His noble purpose.

*Colleen Townsend is the author of numerous books, including* Bold Commitment, *co-authored with her husband, Louis H. Evans, pastor of the Menlo Park Presbyterian Church. Colleen has served on the boards of World Vision, and "One Ministries," a church-related inner-city ministry to the poor.*

# I Can't Get Along Without You, Lord

## Colleen Townsend Evans

How happy are the humble-minded, for the kingdom of Heaven is theirs!
(Matt. 5:3, J.B. Philips)
Blessed are the poor in spirit: for theirs is the kingdom of Heaven. (Matt. 5:3, KJV)

Poor—I can't imagine anyone wanting to be poor; to be totally destitute, in need, anxious, hopeless, frightened. Surely our loving Lord doesn't want this for us? Yet Jesus says that only if we are poor will we be happy: "Blessed are the poor in spirit: for theirs is the kingdom of Heaven."

There were many poor people sitting at the feet of Jesus when He spoke these words, and He always identified himself with them. In fact, He told His followers that as they served the "least of these," His brothers and sisters, they would be serving *Him*. But He wasn't telling the poor in the crowd that day that they had never had it so good. No. Jesus had great compassion for human need, and the sight of the suffering poor grieved Him. It was obvious He was talking about something beyond physical need.

All right, suppose I were in the crowd that came to hear Him speak, and suppose I were poor. I wouldn't have come to get food. He had none. I wouldn't have come for money. He had none. But perhaps I would have come because I needed something else that only Jesus could give me.

Yes, there seems to be a new meaning now in the word *poor*. I had been thinking in terms of the poverty we're trying to eliminate from our world: hunger, starvation, disease, ignorance. But there is another kind of poverty— devastating, if not as visible. There is a poverty of the spirit. And that's what Jesus is talking about in the first Beatitude.

"Blessed are the poor in *spirit*. . . ." This seems to be the center from which the other Beatitudes radiate. For unless we know how poor we are without Christ, we'll never reach out for Him. If we feel we can take care of ourselves, why ask for help—even from God?

## The Happiest People

Come to think of it, the happiest people I know are those who have tried and failed—even hit bottom—and then reached out for help. Realizing their spiritual bankruptcy, they asked Jesus to take over their lives. They entered the Kingdom through the door of their own need, and they were met by God's grace.

They're not only the happiest, but the freest people I've known: free to be, to love, and to let God work through them. They enjoy each moment, with no regrets for yesterday and no worries about tomorrow. They don't have to prove anything: they work because they *want* to, not because the world expects it of them. To me, these people are very rich—not necessarily in material things, but in

90 Fruit from the Vine

the things of the spirit. They possess the peace and joy that come from walking close to God. Yet this route to the Kingdom begins with the painful admission that we are poor and needy. This is the *sine qua non* of our spiritual lives: the most basic fact. We are to trust God, not ourselves, and God means for us to learn that.

For me that learning began during my mid-teens when, without actually seeking it, I had an experience that was both mystical and profound. One evening when I was alone, I went to my room and found myself in the presence of a blinding white light. It was all around me, overwhelming, consuming. I was part of it, and it was part of me. At the core of my being, in my spirit, I felt free and peaceful. I was aware of my oneness with all things, all people, and especially with God.

Since that moment I have never doubted the reality of God or His presence in our human lies. Although that experience wasn't repeated, I still have the strength and assurance it gave me. That was the beginning of my conscious spiritual journey.

For many years I didn't mention that evening to anyone except my mother. In fact, even now I wonder about sharing such an intensely personal incident, for I think we are in trouble when we base our faith upon experience or feeling alone. Yet what we have seen and heard and touched is a valid part of ourselves. For me, that moment was where my pilgrimage began.

In the years that followed I held fast to my faith in God, allowing Him to influence my life but not to guide it; I could do that myself. Then, during my college years, I began to feel a gnawing hunger. There *had* to be more to life than what I saw on the surface. We *had* to do more than go through the motions. There *had* to be meaning, warmth, closeness, love. I was hungry for more of God in my life, but I didn't know where to find Him.

Up to that point my relationship with established religion

had been casual. I had wandered in and out of church. Now I looked to the church to show me the way to God. I joined, I worked, I tithed, I tried, and I found only frustration and weariness. The route of "churchianity" was not for me.

## A Gnawing Hunger

By that time I had gone from college to Hollywood, where I was put under contract to a motion-picture studio and promised a creative career. I thoroughly enjoyed my work: It was fun, exciting, and lucrative, and I loved the people! Materially, my background had been very simple, and for the first time in my life I had some of the things I always thought I wanted—plus glamorous surroundings, stimulating work, and talented friends. Yet underneath the surface of my being—deep down in my spirit—my possessions added up to zero. I had more of everything, but "everything" was not enough. The gnawing hunger was still there.

I felt poor—in a way that had nothing to do with anything external. My poverty was on the inside. True, I had been aware of my spiritual needs for months, but there was always something I could do about them: work harder, try harder, search further. Not anymore. I had run out of things to do. I had done them all, and I was exhausted. And what good were all my efforts? Where did they get me? Spiritually I was bankrupt. Let someone else try.

Someone did. At that most needful time in my life I met a group of young new Christians. They were such warm, real people, and I felt myself being drawn toward their loving concern for me. They became my friends, and I began to hear what they were saying about God.

My friends told me that God was real, but I already knew that. They said there is a God-sized vacuum in each of us; and until it is filled with God, we will never have true peace. I was beginning to know that. But then they told me something I had never known. They told me how to find God! they said I wouldn't find Him by doing good or by working harder. They said I wouldn't find Him through any efforts of my own. They said I would find Him through a Person—through a Person so much like myself that He would understand my needs, yet Someone so thoroughly *God* that He could feed my hungry spirit.

At last I understood. At last I had been shown the Way. My friends urged me to follow it, to give Jesus my impoverished life and let Him make something useful out of it. So I did. It was quiet and simple, and very, very real. I said yes to Jesus Christ, the God I had known to be real— but far away—He came into my life.

What a difference there is between a vague sort of faith and a personal relationship with a living Christ! He has given me direction and a goal, and nothing has ever been quite the same for me. If I had to describe in a few words how my life has been changed by becoming His disciple, I would borrow these words from Jesus: ". . . anyone who keeps his life for himself shall lose it; and anyone who loses his life for me shall find it again" (Matt. 16:25, TLB).

Left to ourselves, we find this world a lonely place. No matter how many friends we have or how big our family, we feel cut off from a warmth and love we can't describe. It's always out there somewhere, until we open our hearts and let the Holy Spirit "in here." The Holy Spirit is a part of God Himself, and He will keep us company as long as we live on this earth.

So the spiritual life begins with our becoming poor in spirit. We place our feet on the first step of the ladder and become children of God. Though Matthew never uses the term "new birth," the Beatitudes teach us what it will be like, and they both begin with "I need."

In our Kingdom-walk we are receivers—doers, too, but receivers first. Yet not all of us accept God's gifts. Some people, because of their pride, cannot reach out and take them. They resent God and they are never happy.

It is neither wealth nor poverty that keeps us out of the Kingdom. It is our pride that falsely tells us we have no need. Pride wants too much and offers too little.

### Humility Has Many Friends

Humility is just the opposite: The humble are *not* proud. They know they need help, so they get it. The Kingdom Jesus established is not to be forced on anyone, but gladly given to those who know their need and are ready to receive from God. Humility is smart enough to know we can't know everything. It listens, and it looks at life through the eyes of others. Humility has many friends because it has time and space in its life for more than itself. The door to its heart is never locked. Humility is thankful for all it has, and because it has received so much, it gives unendingly.

Humility opens the way to God and happiness. Pride stands back, hands at its sides, and says, "No thanks, I can do it myself." Humility comes with hands outstretched.

Thinking about humility reminds me of two wonderful people we met in Edinburgh many, many years ago. Louie and I had gone to Scotland so he could complete his graduate studies at New College. We had spent summers in work camps overseas, but this time we were to be away from our country and our family for two years, and we were expecting our first child.

Louie's adviser and New Testament teacher was Professor James Stewart, a man well-known as a New Testament scholar and a powerful preacher. We went to hear him preach at Saint George's West on our first Sunday in Edinburgh, and after the service we stayed in our seats for a long time, savoring the inspiration his words had given us. He was a man small in stature and gigantic in spirit—a man of natural talents, disciplined mind, and power uniquely born of the Holy Spirit. We were so grateful that Louie was to learn from this man for the next two years.

As great as he was in the pulpit, Professor Stewart was even more impressive as a human being—and in the gentlest, most humane way. We might have felt homesick those first months had it not been for the many kindnesses he and his lovely wife, Rosamund, sent our way. They came to see me in the hospital when our son Dan was born six weeks earlier than expected. They invited us to spend Christmas with them and their family, realizing that this was the first time we had been away from home for the holidays. And then there were the evenings we and our fellow students spent at their house, drinking good tea and asking questions of Professor Stewart late into the night. And Rose pedaling over to our flat on her bicycle with flowers picked from her garden, arriving just in time for a "wee visit" while I nursed the "bairn." (We had a baby a year in Scotland, so there was always a bairn.)

The "gift" that meant the most to us came when little Dan was six weeks old. By that time Louie was filling the pulpit in a little country church in Penicuik every Sunday, and we wanted to have our son baptized there. Louie, as Dan's father, couldn't perform the service, and of course you can guess who we wanted to do it. But we just didn't have the nerve to ask.

Getting to Penicuik wasn't easy. It meant a forty-five minute ride through the Pentland hills—in the middle of winter. A car in postwar Britain was a luxury few of us could afford, so we took a long bumpy ride on a bus. It was too much to ask—warm and generous as Professor Stewart was, he was still a very busy man. A friend of ours offered to do the service, and we gratefully accepted.

On the morning of Dan's baptism, I dressed him in his warmest and best, and the four of us took the long bus ride to Penicuik. It was cold and the roads were icy, so the ride was longer than usual. When we arrived at the church, I was taken to the vestry. Then, at the appropriate moment in our service, I was led down the aisle, holding Dan in my arms. Out of the corner of my eye I thought I recognized a man sitting in the rear of the church. After the sacrament, I turned to walk back down the aisle, and this time I got a better look. I had been right the first time. It was Professor Stewart! Hearing one of our friends mention that Dan was going to be baptized, he had come all the way out on the bus by himself to be there. After the service he slipped away as quietly as he had come. *But he had been there.* In that act, and in countless others like it, he and Rose taught me more about the Christian life and attitude than all his sermons put together. And now these many years later, we have new data that tells us the Stewarts are still giving themselves to others in the same beautiful way. Our youngest son has just returned from studying in Edinburgh, and the highlight of his stay was his friendship with these same two people who walk so humbly with God. (There was however one frustration. Our son James Stewart Evans wanted to learn all he could about his namesake, Professor Stewart, but he could never get him to talk about himself.)

## Pride Doesn't Even Give God a Chance!

To be poor in spirit is to be in touch with our own need. It's uncomfortable—that's why our spiritual need must be filled before we can touch the needs of others. Before we can appreciate the worth of another human being, we must feel that we ourselves are of value. And many of us don't.

It's a funny thing about pride—often it's a cover-up for a low opinion of the self. It's a way of saying, "All right, world, I know nobody can love me, so I'll look after myself!" It doesn't even give God a chance.

I have a friend, a very lovely person, who, when she

was younger, had so little feeling of self-worth that she almost called it quits. She was so desperately in need of self-respect that she was completely unable to give to others. Margot even found it difficult to function as wife and mother, but she covered up her sense of deficiency with a layer of pride. None of us realized how empty she felt inside.

One day Margot felt a mysterious stirring within her. Gently but persistently, it pushed against her pride until it cracked. Without quite understanding what she was doing, Margot reached out for help. She began coming to church for counseling, and when her minister realized how deep her feelings of unworthiness were, he persuaded her to see a sensitive, caring psychiatrist.

It's wonderful how God uses time and people. For many long, tiring months, the minister and the psychiatrist worked with Margot, and through them God was able to bring about a healing in her life.

Margot was driving home from the psychiatrist's office one day after a session that had been a breakthrough— a moment when the light of understanding broke through to her darkened spirit. As she drove through the park, she began to feel warmed by that inner light, and suddenly she found herself saying, "Margot, you're a precious person. You're special." Over and over she said it, until she began to cry. She pulled over, stopped the car, and sat basking in a wonderful new awareness of God's love for her. When Margot started the car to drive home, she did something significant. She reached down and fastened her seatbelt. She had never done that before. Now, in one simple action, she was saying, "God cares for me, and *I* care."

Margot was beginning a whole new life that was totally different from anything she had known. Love—God's love—transformed her into a generous and thoughtful person. Being able to receive made her able to give and, as she looked around, she saw how much she was needed. At last she could look beyond herself to others.

## A Beautiful Postscript

This past year I experienced a beautiful postscript to this story. On a trip west, Louis and I visited a church where we met person after person who told us how much they had been helped by a gifted, caring psychologist on the church staff. She was a woman with amazing sensitivity to their problems. Yes—her name was Margot.

Christians walk humbly with their Lord, or they don't walk the Way. Humility itself can become proud—proud of being loved, proud of serving, proud of achieving. That's when Jesus reminds us of our poverty—to keep us humble. He takes us through one of life's many valleys of humiliation. I don't know how to avoid these valleys—there are no detours along the Way.

There have been valleys for us as a couple—many of them. But there has also been joy—joy in fulfilling of the promise that "every valley shall be exalted" (Isa. 40:4, KJV). It has often been painful for us to be put in touch with our own spiritual need, but it has brought us, and kept us, close to God. And that *is* happiness!

## One of the Family

So to be poor in spirit is to walk humbly with God. But it is also walking humbly with others. When we become part of the Kingdom of God, we join a family and every other person in the Kingdom becomes our brother and sister. From then on, there can be no conflicting loyalties.

The Kingdom is consuming. It is not for the faint-hearted or for those simply "interested in religion." Rather, it is for those ready to begin a new way of life. Part of this new way is that, unlike the world, the Kingdom is not exclusive. It is for all people without respect to race, color, nationality, education, or station in life.

My prayer is: "Lord, I want to walk humbly with You,

and with all Your other children—my brothers and sisters. Then, and only then, will I be ready to go on to the other Beatitudes, like being meek, merciful, and a peacemaker. I need Your gifts so much. I want to learn what it means to be a Christian in the deepest sense, so I come to you with my hands open and outstretched."

Happy are the people who know that without God they are nothing, but that with God working through them they have the strength and power of His love. They have learned the most basic lesson of the spiritual life: to trust God, not themselves. Their humility will come from the very center of their being. It will never allow them to look down on anyone—not even on people who look down on people. And, because humility is real, they will know a bit of Heaven right here on earth.

*In 1982, Father Joseph L. Bernardin, Archbishop of Cincinnati, was called to Chicago, where he soon became Cardinal. First and always a loving pastor, he seeks to bring Christ to people who need Him most, devoting much time to the sick, elderly, and prisoners.*

# God Needs Us Too

## Joseph L. Bernardin

The most important task of the committed Christian is to proclaim the Lord Jesus and His Good News in such a way as to elicit a deep, personal commitment to Him and an acceptance of His message. For like St. Paul, as we heard a moment ago, "We must preach not ourselves, but Jesus Christ as Lord. . ." (II Cor. 4:5). This is the work of evangelization, which always aims at conversion.

There are many reasons why the work of evangelization is so urgent today. Perhaps the most important is that we live in a world dominated by secular and material values. Many people no longer perceive their lives as having a dimension of transcendence. As a result, more and more people have shown signs of apathy and indifference, alienation and hostility—even to the point of no longer practicing their religion and falling away altogether from the faith. At the same time, many other people, even though they go to church less often and sometimes challenge religious authority, retain a religious orientation. Surveys show that they yearn for a closer relationship with God and that they pray frequently.

## Committed Christians and Evangelism

Fortunately, there are also many people who are truly committed to the Lord. They are totally dedicated people, very much involved in the life of the Church, who give a marvelous witness to God's love and mercy in their daily lives. These good people, who often go unnoticed, are more aware than ever of the need to make the Lord known to those who have turned away from Him and those who are searching for Him; to show in a concrete and credible way that the Christian faith is as relevant as it ever was; that, without faith in the Lord, even the greatest of human accomplishments will bring little of lasting value. Committed Christians have come to the realization that, in the face of this great need for evangelization, they cannot simply sit back and do nothing. While the grace of faith and conversion surely comes from God, we are the human instruments God uses to draw people closer to Himself.

How do we proclaim Jesus Christ and His good news? How do we do it in our time—in the environment in which we live—in a way that will be effective? This is a vital question for everyone, because the task of preaching Christ and His gospel is the responsibility of everyone who belongs to the community of faith we call the Church. I can assure you it is an important question for me. There are times when I wonder how much effect my ministry really has. As you know, I minister in Cincinnati. Now, the Archbishop of Cincinnati, no matter who he might be, has always had a high standing in the community. My name, for example, is on every invitation list for civic and community functions. People are very kind to me and they give me a respectful hearing. But are they really listening to what I am saying?

Are their lives affected by it? Do they understand that the words I preach are not my own? Do they look beyond those words, beyond the sacred rites I perform, and see the Lord Jesus? I have the uneasy feeling that many do not. If so, my ministry is less fruitful than it should be. So what do I do? And what do you, who are united with me in Christian faith, do?

**Teenagers' Observation**

The greatest need at this time, for each of us as individuals and for all of us as a community of faith, is to live out our faith in our daily lives. To put it another way, our lives must be so gospel-oriented that people will be convinced that we are believers. In late 1977, George Gallup found in a survey that, while America's teenagers are quite religious in certain ways, they are turned off by churches and organized religion. A comment typical of this age group was: "Churchgoers have high morals, but they're not Christians—they're spiritually shallow." And another comment was: "Religion should be an exciting experience— but you'd never know it in most churches you go to." Admittedly, this survey was of teenagers. But such attitudes affect all age groups. I talk with and receive letters from many middle-aged and elderly people who tell me the same things. There is a tendency at times to write all this off by saying that such people do not have the faith or, in the case of younger people, that they are immature. But this response is not adequate.

Books of the New Testament like the Acts of the Apostles and the epistles tell us a great deal about the early Christians, those who lived at a time when personal witnesses to Jesus and His ministry were still alive. The most evident phenomenon is the radical change that took place in their lives after they converted to the Lord and were baptized. And it was that change—in the way they lived, the way they incarnated in their day-to-day lives the teaching of Jesus—more than what they said, that impressed their neighbors. "See how those Christians love one another." This became the distinctive mark of the early faith community. This is what caused others to sit up and take notice and ultimately join the community themselves.

We should not really be surprised. One of the most beautiful and revealing utterances of the Lord is His final discourse to the apostles, found in chapters 14-17 of John's Gospel. Jesus clearly states that love is at the very heart of the Christian life. The reason is that love is at the very heart of God's life. As a matter of fact, John, in his first epistle, states quite simply that "God is love" (I John 4:8). In the gospel discourse Jesus speaks of the love that unites Him and His Father. It is because of this love that Jesus is totally submissive to His Father's will. It was this love which prompted Jesus to say in the garden of Gethsemane, when His impending passion and death for us caused Him to experience sorrow and distress: "My Father, if it is possible, let this cup pass me by. Still let it be done as You would have, not as I" (Matt. 26:39).

To be faithful to our call as Christians, we must reflect in our own lives that divine love of the Father, Son and Holy Spirit of which we have been the beneficiaries. And we do that by living lives totally in accord with God's will as revealed by Jesus and handed on to us by His Church. Listen again to the words of Jesus: "As the Father has loved Me, so I have loved you. Live on in My love. All this I tell you that My joy may be yours and your joy may be complete. This is My commandment: love one another as I have loved you" (John 15:9-12).

What does such love demand of us in more specific terms? Many things. Paul spelled it out well for the Corinthians when he said, "Love is patient; love is kind. Love is not jealous, it does not put on airs, it is not snobbish. Love is never rude, it is not self-seeking. It is not prone to anger;

neither does it brood over injuries. Love does not rejoice in what is wrong but rejoices with the truth. There is no limit to love's forbearance, to its trust, its hope, its power to endure" (I Cor. 13:4-7). Let us apply those criteria to ourselves. Are we truly patient with our family, our friends, the people with whom we work, our neighbors? Do we make a special effort to say a kind word to them, to show them through some appropriate gesture or in some other way that we care, especially if they are older, or lonely, or ill or incapacitated?

What about people whose skin is not the color of our own? Do we really acknowledge their human dignity? Do we truly accept them as equals, or do we hold back in some way? As citizens, do we use our influence, especially our vote, to elect officials committed to justice and to support legislation that responds to the legitimate needs and aspirations of others, especially the poor and oppressed? Are we sufficiently committed—in our families, in our communities, in our churches—to focusing our attention on the well-being of others and placing the common good before our own? Or are we too self-seeking?

### Hiding Behind a Facade?

Do we look for the truth through study, prayerful reflection, and openness to God's word? Or do we tenaciously hold on to our own ideas and whims, giving them a status—sometimes almost an infallibility—which they do not deserve? Instead of seeking truth and giving people the benefit of the doubt, are we quick to spread rumors which reach us? Do our religious acts really represent interior goodness on our part, or have they become a facade hiding attitudes unworthy of us as followers of the Lord?

### Will Your Evangelizing Efforts Bear Fruit?

Beyond all this, are we willing to show a great concern and compassion for others—not only by particular acts on their behalf, but by being present to them? Often, people's wants and needs are much less complex than we might imagine. They know we cannot solve all their problems or answer all their questions. Often they already know the answer; they may even know there is no immediate solution to their problem. More than anything else, they look to us for our presence as loving, caring, and forgiving people. They want help in coping with their pain and frustration. They look for understanding; they want a sensitive and consoling response to their hurt feelings. They are looking for someone who will pray with them, someone whose presence will remind them that, no matter what their difficulties, God really does love them and care for them; someone whose presence will give them the assurance that they will never be abandoned. Are we willing to be present to our friends in this way, even when doing so demands patience and effort on our part? Admittedly, these are hard questions, but they must be asked if we are to come to grips with our personal standing in the sight of God and determine whether our conversion to the Lord has been real. As I intimated earlier, the answers to these questions will ultimately determine whether or not our evangelizing efforts will be fruitful.

I am convinced that living the Christian life in all its integrity demands complete surrender to the Lord. If we truly believe in God and if we believe that Jesus is God's Son, then we must adore Him. We adore or worship in many ways: through the public prayer and rites of the Church and our own private prayer, through various gestures that symbolize our dependence on God. But in the final analysis, external actions will have meaning only if inwardly we surrender ourselves completely to the Lord.

Adoration is one's personal response to God's love. Ideally, therefore, it is the highest and most intense act of which we are capable. To adore is to abandon ourselves completely into the loving hands of God: "Lord, do with me what you will." It is easy to say that we have surrendered ourselves in this way; most of us assert this every day in our public acts of worship and in our private prayer. But true surrender—in terms of our daily lives, in terms of our thinking and acting, and in terms of our priorities—is much more difficult. We are human beings, and, despite our best intentions and efforts, we frequently hold back; we lack the courage to be different, to suffer ridicule or persecution for Christ's sake; we hold on desperately to false hopes. The effort to abandon ourselves to the Lord—to adore Him in the most perfect way possible—is a lifelong task. It demands our constant attention if we are to be truly converted to the Lord, and if we are to be credible witnesses to His goodness and love.

As a pastor who has a great love for you and whose only concern is the spiritual well-being of all people, I urge you personally always to remain close to the Lord. Without fear or hesitation let us, together, surrender ourselves completely to Him. Every day may we converse with Him through prayer. Let us share with Him our innermost thoughts, our hopes and aspirations, our anxieties and frustrations, our successes and failures, our weaknesses and sins. May we never hold anything back, because nothing should be off-limits. Let there be no part of our lives that we reserve exclusively for ourselves; let us open all to Him.

**Are Your Prayers a Monologue?**

We must not let our prayer become a monologue. We must also listen to the Lord as He speaks to us through the scriptures, through the Church's preaching and teaching, through our worship as a community of faith, through the lives of those who are close to us, through the signs of the times. We must make time every day to pray. This time is a very sacred moment when nothing should interfere with our conversation with Jesus. But prayer does not end with these sacred, privileged moments. The entire day must become a time of prayer, in the sense that it must be spent entirely in the presence of the Lord. At all times, in our moments of joy and sadness, work and recreation, we should be aware of the Lord's presence in our lives.

### We Are Literally God's Children

We are like children who play in the presence of their parents. Children become very engrossed in what they are doing when they play, and frequently they may not think of their parents at all. But instinctively they know they are there, always loving them and always ready to help and protect them. All they need do is reach out and their parents' loving hands are always there to grasp theirs. So it is with us who, regardless of age or background or sophistication, are quite literally God's children. My dear brothers and sisters in the Lord! May you never forget your call to proclaim the Lord Jesus and His gospel to all people. May your personal interests, no matter how legitimate, never become obstacles to your witness. Rather, in all that you do, at work and at home and at play, reflect the goodness, the love and mercy, the understanding and compassion of the Lord Himself.

*For many years Harold Blake Walker was senior pastor of the First Presbyterian Church in Evanston, Illinois, and is now Pastor Emeritus. Among his pastoral duties, he found time to write a widely-syndicated inspirational column for the Chicago* Tribune Magazine.

# The Other Side of Sorrow

## Harold Blake Walker

So you have sorrow now, but I will see you again and your hearts will rejoice, and no one will take your joy from you. (John 16:22, RSV)

**M**ost of us are reluctant to accept the fact that death is the inevitable end of life. Possibly it is our reluctance to consider the inevitability of death that accounts for our being so surprised and shocked by it.

At one time or another all of us share the bewilderment of Ezekiel when his beloved wife died. He wrote poignantly, "I sat overwhelmed." We, too, have been overwhelmed by the loss of loved ones and in that moment of loss, death becomes starkly real.

Jesus was altogether realistic about the inevitability of death. He had numbered the days of His own life and measured the impact of His death on the lives of His disciples. "You have sorrow now," He said to them as if to affirm the fact that they could not escape the pain of loss. The disciples, in very human fashion, could not accept the idea that Jesus would be taken from them. His death, despite all He said to them seemed incredible. In somewhat the same way we confront death, our own and that of others, with feelings of incredulity.

There is, however, a certain wisdom for life which involves the quiet acceptance of the evitable and thoughtful contemplation of it. I do not mean to suggest a morbid wallowing in sentimental sadness, but rather a forthright consideration of what should be done when death comes. There are some mundane matters for thought. It is important, for example, for each of us to have an up-to-date will, and to provide instructions concerning the funeral and the type of place of burial. Somebody needs to know what our wishes are; otherwise a heavy burden is imposed on those left behind to make decisions we should have made ourselves.

### Overwhelmed For A Time

At best it is difficult for those who suffer the loss of someone they have loved dearly. They are "overwhelmed" for a while at least. St. Augustine, meditating sadly on the death of a beloved friend wrote, "I could not see how the sun would shine while half of my soul lay dead." If we have lost loved ones we understand precisely what Augustine meant; half of ourselves seems dead, the sun does not seem warm and the stars no longer shine. We feel bereft, wondering if we will be able to pick up the pieces of our lives again.

Even though we have planned together for the eventuality of death, we know that when the time comes we will, as Jesus said, "have sorrow now." There will be tears, and why not? Tears are the natural response to the death of one we have loved dearly. I am sure it is a mistake not to express our honest feelings. If we do not express grief, we repress it, bury it in the subconscious where it festers. It may well develop someday into a psychological problem.

It is suggestive to notice that after the death of his beloved, Ezekiel sat for a while "overwhelmed," and I dare say he shed tears. He did not, however, remain willfully inert in his sadness. On the contrary, he picked up the threads of his life and pushed on, honoring his loved one with a creative response to her death. He exposed his life to the world around him and committed himself to the task of saving his people from their folly. His greatness as a prophet was his response to the agony of his loss.

Gladys Tabor, who suffered the loss of a dear one, was "overwhelmed" for a while. She shut herself away in her grief. In that state, she wrote, "I had no sense of my loved one. It was as if I were the only person in the world." She was depressed and she depressed everyone around her. Then she recognized the folly of her willful sadness and began to live with a "determination not to be miserable." She exposed herself to the world around her, "felt the excitement of the first snowflakes" and laughed at a child, "lugging a pink rabbit around." Then she began to know that the one she had loved still was with her in spirit.

### A Fellowship of Spirit on the Other Side of Sorrow

That, I suspect is what Jesus wanted to convey to His disciples when He said, "So you have sorrow now, but I will see you again." It was a striking affirmation of His faith that there is a fellowship of the spirit *on the other side of sorrow.* He was altogether certain that death would not end the saga of His life. If His disciples did not shut themselves up in grief they would meet His spirit in the quiet of the night and know that wherever they were gathered in the service of the Highest, there He would be also.

Some years ago, Professor David Roberts of Union Theological Seminary died in the prime of his life. He was a man of great promise, devoted to his work and to his family. He had a small daughter who often played with a four-year-old boy who lived next door. The boy was not told of the death of Professor Roberts, but he missed seeing the friendly man. He asked his mother what had happened to Dr. Roberts and she replied that he was with God. Whereupon the boy said, "Oh, then he is still real."

The great and exciting affirmation of the Christian faith is that those who have gone on are still real. As Jesus put the matter, "I will see you again." He knew that if His disciples could understand that even after death He still would be real they would not blunder into despair or flounder in futility. They would miss Him, to be sure, but they would understand He would not leave them alone.

In the play by Channing Pollock entitled *Shining Armor,* the action of the play takes place on two levels of the stage. Archie, the husband, dies toward the end of the story, parting sadly from his beloved wife. In the closing scene on the lower stage, his wife, tired and weary, is resting in the little home she and Archie had built together. As she rests, darkness falls and she slips over the border from life to death. But as darkness shrouds the lower stage, the upper stage glows with light. There stands Archie, his face wreathed in smiles and his arms outstretched. Out of the shadows steps the woman he loves. He reaches out his hand to her and she links her arm in his in the old way they knew, and they go on together into eternity.

To be sure, the scene is symbolic, and it suggests in a striking way what Jesus meant when He said, "I will see you again." It is a magnificent symbolic portrayal of the Christian hope that even in death, those we love still are real. "Now abideth faith, hope and love and the greatest of these is love," for love is eternal and it holds God's answer to the lonely years.

### Out of the Depths to Eventual Rejoicing

There is sustaining strength and hope in the conviction that through all the agonies and losses of life we do not walk alone. If we dare to say in the midst of sorrow, "I'm going back," back to the tasks of life, back to pick up the pieces of life and go on, we discover that both our loved ones and Christ are still real. The ringing affirmation, "I will see you again" is the source of our hope and our trust in life.

Jesus went on to insist that even after the loss of one greatly loved "your hearts will rejoice." It was not a matter of whistling in the dark, but rather a great affirmation of the fact that the grace and the love of God are available to us in our need. If we lose those we have loved, we find the love and strength of God. Through the years of my ministry I have witnessed that fact over and over again. I have watched men and women moving out of the depths of sorrow and grief to rejoicing in hope.

Jackson Burns, once a minister in Cambridge, Mass., says that on an occasion after he had preached a sermon based on the Twenty-third Psalm, a mathematics professor at Harvard pointed out that in the beginning of the Psalm the author spoke of God in the third person, as "The Lord," and as "He." But when the Psalmist reached the point where he spoke of the "valley of the shadow," he began to speak directly to God: "For Thou art with me; Thy rod and Thy staff they comfort me." And so he continued through the Psalm.

To the professor the change seemed insignificant. It suggested that often when we blunder into the "valley of the shadow of death," we find God in more personal and intimate ways than we have known Him before. We discover the tender ministries of the Comforter Jesus promised, and we become aware that God has not forgotten our need.

There is, I am sure, a two-fold source of our rejoicing as we emerge from our grief. The first, as we have noted, is the discovery of God's sustaining grace. The second is the emerging confidence that God deals gently with those who have gone beyond our reach. The understanding that all is well is reason for both gratitude and rejoicing. In the days of long ago when the town crier called out in the night, "All is well," the townspeople must have felt assured and secure.

## In God's Care and Keeping

So, like the Shunammite woman whose son died suddenly, we are blessed by the knowledge that in God's care and keeping, "All is well." The Shunammite woman set out to find Elisha, the prophet, after her son's death. When he saw her coming, he sent his servant to ask the woman, "Is it well with thee? Is it well with thy husband? Is it well with the child?" She replied, "It is well." It took courage and faith to say that!

There is a vast difference in the way people deal with the loss of loved ones. There are some who find no comfort or strength for their agony because they never have reached out to God in faith. They blunder into resentment or bitterness or both. "Why did this happen to me?" they ask petulantly. They cannot say, "All is well," because they cannot believe it is so. They seem determined to be miserable.

On the other hand, there are men and women who, in the midst of their pain quite naturally lean their lives on the strength of God because they are accustomed to do so. They have not doubt that "All is well" with those they have loved and lost awhile. So, after the shock of their loss has faded, they turn back to life with both gratitude and enthusiasm. Often, in grateful response for God's mercies, they seek to serve God through service to others.

Emily Bronte put her finger on the way the faithful move out of sorrow into newness of life. She wrote of "My darling pain,"

"That wounds and sears
And wrings a blessing out from tears."

Carl Sandburg sounds a similar note in his lines,

"One more arch of stars,
In the night of our mist,
In the night of our tears."

The faithful find a blessing coming "out from tears," and "one more arch of stars" flowing from "the night of our tears."

As if Jesus wished to emphasize the possibility of rejoicing even after loss, He went on to insist "and no one will take your joy from you." Gladys Tabor sensed the truth when she wrote, "I do not know why I was destined to walk alone for so long. I no longer ask. I accept this as I accept rain and wind and weather. I reach out to life with an open hand. And on Christmas eve, I find it easy to say with a grateful and tranquil heart the words I have said down the years on this night: 'God rest you merry gentlemen, let nothing you dismay.' "

## One Day We Will Understand the Mystery

Life and death are two halves of a single whole. One day we shall understand the mystery, but not yet. At the moment we have no choice but to journey in faith, remembering that God said, "Let there be light," and there was light. Meanwhile, until the light dawns, we live by faith and prove the truth of the Christian revelation by exhibiting its meaning in the way we respond to what we cannot avoid.

We need to live only one hour, one day at a time in confidence that God is able to see us through the present moment if we do not weight it down with fears for the long future. Each hour of each day we can prove the truth of the Christian revelation and make our witness to the fact that no one can take from us the joy of living and contributing to the common life around us. As one man said after the loss of his wife, "I will not add to the world's woe and sadness by anything I do or say. There is enough hurt in the world without adding mine." So, hour by hour and day by day he poured out his life in a ministry of helpfulness and other concern.

### From Tragedy to Triumph and Sorrow to Rejoicing

It is in such fashion that we transform tragedy into triumph and sorrow into rejoicing. As we turn our backs on ourselves and our faces toward the needs of others we find life deeply rewarding. To be sure, there will be times when, quite unaccountably, we come upon a doleful morning when we say to ourselves, "How can I face another day?" But with only one hour, one minute to manage, we can cope. As one woman said, "I got up with such a hopeless feeling that I made grape jelly to share with my friends."

"Blessed are they that mourn," not because they feel the agony of loss, as of course they do, but because they "shall be comforted." And the word comfort means "sustained with strength," strength for the hours and the days. As they mourn they identify with the world's sorrow and pain and find their hope, not in adding to the world's woe and sadness, but in testifying to the truth of the Christian revelation by exhibiting its meaning by the way they respond to what they cannot avoid.

The disciples suffered acutely as they watched from a safe distance the crucifixion of their Lord. They were overwhelmed, bereft, and yet before the saga was finished they were on the march again, preaching, teaching, building a church, honoring the Master by their magnificent response to His death and to the discovery He still was real, in death as in life. They remembered His soft-spoken words, "So you have sorrow now, but I will see you again and your hearts will rejoice, and no one will take your joy from you."

*Before assuming the pastorate of Chicago's Monumental Baptist Church (of which he is now Pastor Emeritus), Dr. D. E. King served on the faculties of both Southern and Northern Baptist Seminaries, as well as Alabama State A & M. He has traveled the world over on preaching missions.*

# Squirm Like A Worm or Fly Like An Eagle

## D. E. King

In his account of the resurrection of Jesus, Luke tells how two of Jesus' disciples were returning from Jerusalem to the village of Emmaus on that first Easter Sunday. On their way home these bedraggled, brow-beaten, down-hearted disciples were discussing the horrible, brutal things that had happened to Jesus over the weekend. As they journeyed, Jesus joined them. But, because He was in a disguised form, they did not know Him. Jesus asked the two what they were talking about. Here's how Luke describes the scene:

"Then one of them, whose name was Cleopas, answering said unto Him, 'Art Thou only a stranger in Jerusalem, and hast not known the things which are come to pass there in these days?' And He said unto them, 'What things?' " (Luke 24:18-19).

Cleopas then detailed to Jesus the atrocious things that had been inflicted on the mortal body of his Lord. And there He stood before them in His resurrected form because *His immortality had risen above mortal things.* Every Easter should cause us to ponder the truth of such immortal power over mortal things.

## Eternity is Embedded in All of Us

Let us begin with the *primacy of immortality in human life.* The resurrection of the body of Jesus was a climactic miracle to mortal minds. But it was a normal act for Jesus Christ. He lived on earth in divine nature, and thereby kept the immortal side of His life in the ascendancy. That is, He never allowed Himself to be tangled in tangibles. For that reason, even before He was crucified, He accomplished things that seemed utterly beyond the range of mortal powers. His secret was this. *He was ever conscious that immortality has always resided in human nature.* It is that divine quality which God breathed into man's nostrils in creation; and man became a living immortal soul. God breathed immortality into mortality. Hence, eternity is imbedded in the very fiber of human personality. But, somehow, the human race, through the ages, allowed mortality to have the ascendancy. Thus, we became dwarfed and unaware of our immortal powers. We, therefore, have built our lives on the ground-plan of the natural, the mortal or materialism. That is the reason the whole world in on the verge of spiritual bankruptcy!

But Jesus was ever conscious of the primacy or supremacy and authority of the secular. He could thereby mobilize His immortal powers over against the abundance of mortal things. Never did He yield to the limitations or the restrictions of the mortal. For that reason, He could rise above mortal things, and perform such miracles as turning water into wine, feeding five thousand people from a boy's lunch of five barley loaves and two small fishes; walking on the water, quelling a storm, casting out demons, healing all manner of diseases, and raising the dead. When the disciples marvelled at these miracles, Jesus assured them that "these things shall you do also; and greater things than these shall ye do." But to do those things we must rise above mortal things. We must ever be conscious of the primacy of immortality, and keep it in the ascendancy.

### The Temporary is Always Replaced by the Permanent

In the second place, the *temporary* is always replaced by the *permanent*. Mortality is temporary; immortality is permanent, eternal. "We know in part," says Paul, "but when that which is perfect is come, than that which is in part shall be done away." This is even true in the natural order of things. Take metamorphosis, for instance. This is a process by which some creatures change from one form to another. In the process they lose their original identity. One such creature is the tadpole. In its original temporary form, it is a slimy, black legless water creature. But when its permanent form arrives, its entire structure is changed and it is transformed into a leaping, croaking frog. Ask that creature that has risen from his tadpoleness into a frog, what happened to its original things? It would ask, "What things?"

Another creature is the caterpillar. In its original form it is a frightening, crawling worm. When you see it crawling along, it is going to pick up its wings. When it puts them on, it is transformed into a beautiful butterfly. Ask it what happened to the frightening things of its wormness? And it will ask, "What things?" Likewise, in his reference to mortal human life, Paul says, "We shall all be changed. For this corruptible shall put on incorruption, and this mortal shall put on immortality." This is the reason the two disciples of Emmaus did not recognize Jesus. At first, in His disguised appearance, He looked like a mortal being, a stranger. When He inquired of them what their conversation was all about, Cleopas asked, "Haven't you heard of the things that happened to Jesus of Nazareth?" Jesus asked, "What things?" He had risen above the memory of those mortal things that were even done to Him. He could do this because His life was invested with a permanence entirely out of proportion to temporary phenomena.

## Would You Really Rather Be a Worm?

But humanity, generally is somewhat like the butterfly in Charlotte Perkins Gilman's poem, "A Conservative." The poet came upon a beautiful butterfly with wings of black and red hues. It was lamenting the process that had transformed it from a worm into a creature with wings, which it neither desired nor appreciated. When the purpose of its gorgeous appendages was explained to it, it retorted:

> I do not want to fly,
> I only want to squirm!
> And he drooped his wings dejectedly
> But still his voice was firm;
> I do not want to be a butterfly,
> I want to be a worm.

Most people are like that. They are willing to agree with the Negro Spiritual that "All God's chillun got wings," and they want to get to heaven to try on their wings and fly all over God's Heaven. But here on earth they are quite content to be pedestrian souls, asking nothing more of nature than enough mortal power to labor, to strive and to wait. They do not want *to mount up on wings as eagles.* They are quite content to be earthbound to the temporary. That is the reason why He said to Mary and Martha after He raised Lazarus from the dead, "Loose him and let him go."

Now where do we get the power to rise above mortal things? How may we reproduce and experience the self-

forgetfulness of Christ in our own lives. Jesus revealed the
secret when He said, "With men it is impossible; but with
God all things are possible." The Apostle Paul reproduced
and experienced the grace of self-forgetfulness. Note the
atrocious things inflicted upon Him. He lists them, including
his experience of being crucified with Christ. Yet, he shouts,
"But what things were gain to me, I counted loss for Christ,
that I may know Him and the power of His resurrection."
Then He adds, "This one things I do, forgetting those things
which are behind, and reaching forth unto those things
which are before, I press toward the mark for the prize
of the high calling of God in Christ Jesus."

## Oh, I Wish We Could Do That!

Oh, I wish we could do that! I wish the people of the
Middle East would do that. I wish they would forget the
duel between two half brothers, Ishmael and Isaac, the
duel that is still raging between the Arabs and the Jews.
But why go that far. Come closer home. I wish we would
forget the Civil War between the North and the South,
the war which is still raging between black and white. When
those atrocious things which inflame racism are brought
up, I pray that we will rise above them in the risen power
of Christ and ask, "What things?"

Well, you ask, how can this be done? It can be done
because the immortal life of Christ is implicit in us all.
But our souls have become so absorbed in merely *terrestrial*
concerns that they have lost their *celestial* powers. As we
yield to the attraction of things seen, we become blind
to things unseen. As we succumb to the lusts of the flesh,
we become insensitive to the power of the Spirit. When
we become hypnotized by the surface of mortal things,
our upward, seeking immortal impulse, which is native to
the soul, becomes atrophied.

We can only win our souls, and help our spirits emerge

triumphantly by realizing the primacy and authority of immortality in our lives here and now. Through Jesus Christ our Lord, life can be redeemed from a "thingmatized" existence and built to a heavenly scale of immortality. Then, when death comes to claim the mortal, we shall have no regrets, knowing that Christ has brought immortality to light. We shall rise above mortal things with the view that Christ has dominion over all who live in the power of an endless life, knowing that our souls are beyond the reach of death's vandal hands.

Therefore, when mortal things come along and try to distract us, we too can ask in the grace of self-forgetfulness, "What things?"

*After earning his Ph.D. in Philosophy from Columbia University, Paul Nowell Elbin spent most of his adult life as President of West Liberty State College in West Virginia. He was an ordained Presbyterian minister and author of nine books.*

# Take Hold of Life and Live Every Minute!

## Paul Nowell Elbin

*Hard-hats—Do Not Enter!* So read a sign at the entrance to a construction project. But I observed that despite the sign, it was necessary for many men to enter that area every day.

The men, of course, were hard-hat construction workers. They recognized the dangers involved in high-rise construction projects, and they knew how to go about their work with a maximum of protection and a minimum of fear. As both symbol and means of safety, each man wore a steel helmet designed to protect him from sudden danger.

Other kinds of people work in other kinds of hard-hat areas: firemen, policemen, physicians, nurses, mine rescue teams, men in military service, airplane pilots, etc.

In a larger sense all of us spend our lives in a hard-hat area—*life itself.* We never know when we may be hit by unkindness, ingratitude, jealousy, hatred, envy, financial loss, unemployment, accident, illness, bereavement, or death.

There are two ways of reacting to the realization that life, all of it, is an area of constant hazard.

One way is to avoid as much of life as possible. The inhibited, the timid, the cowardly are tempted to bypass as much of life as they can. So they avoid people for fear of being hurt, avoid responsibility for fear of being criticized, avoid ambition for fear of failing, avoid hope for fear of disappointment, and avoid attempts at friendship for fear of being rebuffed.

It must be evident that there are only two means of complete escape by which human beings can avoid the burdens of living. One is suicide. The other is insanity.

Either may follow refusal or inability to enter the wide circle of life boldly with a maximum of protection and a minimum of fear. Suicide or insanity is the logical and final stage of retreat from life.

The second possible way of reacting to the reality of life is to put on the hard-hat of faith in life's possibilities and to challenge life. This means to give life all you have. St. Paul, who was known for practicing what he preached, advised: "Take unto you the whole armor of God, that you may be able to withstand in the evil day, and having done all, *to stand!*" (Eph. 6:13, KJV).

No man knows when he undertakes something worthwhile whether or not he will succeed. A mother bears a child not knowing whether the child will become a blessing or a curse. A man establishes a business not knowing whether it will make him rich or bankrupt. A surgeon begins a lifesaving operation not knowing whether the result will be life or death. Clearly, the best approach to life is to undertake boldly what ought to be done and to do so with maximum protection and minimum fear.

The answer to fear is faith and courage—the hard-hat elements of maximum protection. But in difficult situations, doing is not as easy as knowing.

John Galsworthy observed that courage is more important

than love. But courage is an aspect of love. Faith, hope, and love combine to supply the courage that transforms the wish into the act, the prayer into the answer, the creed into the deed, the vision into the accomplishment. Calvary completed the Sermon on the Mount.

"Happiness at its deepest and best," wrote Harry Emmerson Fosdick, "is not the portion of a cushioned life which never struggled, overpassed obstacles, bore hardships, or adventured into sacrifices for costly aims. A heart of joy is never found in luxurious coddled lives, but in men and women . . . who have tempered their souls in fire."

### Happiness Cannot Be Guaranteed

A person who wants to live happily begins by recognizing the facts of life. The most obvious fact is that life comes to us without desire or effort on our part. Life is a "free" gift, without pre-agreed terms or conditions. Until we arrive at the age of independent decision, we cannot even reject life.

The second fact is that the gift of life carries no guarantee that life will be easy or difficult. This is not to say that life is what we make it. There are too many formative and limited factors. But a person who expects life to provide only wanted experiences assumes a provision not in the Giver's contract.

Though the ingredients of happiness are not the same for all people, all people want to be happy in their chosen way. The pursuit of happiness, Thomas Jefferson believed, is a God-given right no man may rightly deny another.

But not to deny is not the same as to guarantee. Since the Creator allowed a very wide range of freedom for human beings, He could not create beings who would be bubbly happy all the time. Neither God nor man can force happiness on an unwilling or foolish person.

The question every person has to face eventually is this: Can I manage to find happiness in life's mixture of good and evil, life and death?

Beethoven is a marvelous example of a man who could and did. He was only 28 years old when his hearing began to seriously deteriorate. Such an experience would be difficult enough for anyone, but for the gifted young composer-pianist, it threatened the very meaning of life. His struggle was bitter, intense, lengthy. Suicide became a possibility.

After three years Beethoven had made his decision. He concluded a letter about his approaching deafness: "I will seize fate by the throat; most assuredly it shall not get me wholly down—oh, it is so beautiful to live life a thousandfold!"

Thereafter in scores of musical outpourings, Beethoven restated the travail of his soul, the return journey from darkness to light. Even when he could no longer hear anything he had written or anything he played, he continued to make music—the glorious music that will always identify Ludwig van Beethoven as a man who combined good and evil, life and death, in such a manner as to give value and purpose to life.

For twenty-six years after his hearing began its tragic decline, Beethoven continued to pour out the symphonies, sonatas, and concertos that will forever interpret man's spirit to man. Before his years came to an end, he had evolved a philosophy of universal significance: the belief that one must find *"joy in the struggle."*

How true it is! Moments of freedom from struggle are not common. It is a struggle to raise a family, pay the bills, keep healthy, anticipate old age, maintain decency, create beauty, live with honor. But if struggle is accepted as a normal condition of life, not as a surprising intruder, it can be handled with a joy that is distinctively human.

Though the contract for one human life does not

guarantee happiness, the ingredients are all around and
within us. No one can or will, however, combine them for
us. We do that for ourselves, or it is not done.

The happiest people are those who accept, gratefully and
cheerfully, the obvious fact that life in the flesh will end
for each of us on some unknown date, just as childhood
blended into adolescence, and as adolescence gave way
to adulthood. We all live on borrowed time, no one more
than another.

### Attitudes Determine Everything

Yes, attitudes really determine almost everything. No one
who has studied human nature or human psychology has
failed to be impressed by the direct relationship between
our attitudes and what we are in mind, body, and spirit.

The person who is habitually happy is not so idealistic
as not to recognize that there is a negative for every positive.
To recognize that in this world there are both truth and
falsehood, purity and impurity, justice and injustice, is
essential to mature thinking. To dwell on either the positive
or the negative to the virtual exclusion of the other, is
to deny reality. Neither the Pollyanna nor the misanthrope
interprets the world as it really is. One can be sensitive
to happy things, to beauty, to kindness, to what Tennyson
called "the sunnier side of doubt," without neglecting or
ignoring the reverse.

Anyone who wants to live happily will do well to explore
his sensitivities. Spiritually, emotionally, intellectually, we
live by the things to which we become sensitive. . . by lessons
of experience, by the deductions of thought—by earnest
desire, by sincere prayer—by all these ways, we purify and
elevate life. We discover eventually that sensitivities can
be shaped and directed. While childhood environment is
only slightly affected by our choices, *after* childhood we
determine our own environment—by what we choose to

read, to study, to hear on the radio, what we watch on television, or to discuss with other people.

Color photography can shape sensitivity to the world's beauty. The discovery of white clouds against a blue sky, morning fog deep in a valley, spring blossoms in the park, silken curls on a baby, a smile of satisfaction observed on Mother's Day—these are forms of beauty reinforced and preserved on film.

When people travel a country lane, do they see only narrow roads and untended fences? Or do they see redbud trees in bloom, happy children at play, sheep grazing in safety?

When people are confronted with flagrant injustice, does their sensitizing apparatus go to work? Or are they conveniently disposed to pass by "on the other side"?

When a person's kindness is repaid with indifference or hostility, he can react in the spirit of the father who advised his son: "My boy, treat everybody with politeness, even those who are rude to you. Remember that you show courtesy to others not because they are gentlemen, but because you are one."

It is essential that we find *something to reverence* in life. That is the key to the life that is free and full. For all religious people, God is the primary object and inspiration for reverence. Christians reverence God and the Truth incarnated in Jesus Christ.

Life has value and meaning for men and women who have something to reverence, but if they make a habit of burying their lives with fears and frustrations, pessimism eventually will take over.

All sorts of people in unlikely circumstances have proved that life can be beautiful. What a pity then that so many people waste the gift of life by walking mainly under clouds and by slamming doors on beauty and goodness.

*Dr. John Claypool is pastor of St. Luke's Episcopal Church in Birmingham, Alabama, and a former pastor of the Second Baptist Church in Lubbock, Texas. He is also an eloquent speaker and popular with students on campus. This message is one I have shared often with friends.*

# It All Depends

## John R. Claypool

"Two men looked through the self-same bars. One saw mud, the other stars." How can that be? Here are two people looking at the same identical situation, yet one keeps looking down at the lowest and muddiest of what is there, while the other keeps looking up at the splendors that surround the stars. What is it that causes one person to gravitate to the ugly and grim, while another concentrates on the beauty and grace?

I don't suppose there is any one simple answer to that. Perhaps we could by acknowledging that the creatures doing the looking through the bars really are unique in all the world. We human species have been given the gift of interpretation. We don't just perceive reality. We are also given the power to evaluate it, to arrange it in a way that is in relation to other things. We don't simply look on events with a kind of automatic response. The big word for it is self-transcendence. We stand over against things. We have this vantage point, and from that vantage point we tend to give certain values, put price tags. We have the power to name what events are, to name other realities, to decide what they will mean to us, and how we will relate our lives to them. Therefore, the two men looking through the bars do have the freedom to choose. They could select the *lowest* from that scene or they could opt for the *highest*. Our answer than begins with the fact that we are basically "homo interpretatus." But why, if we have the gift of interpretation, do some people always gravitate *down* and other people gravitate *up*?

### Are We Entitled to Life—Or Is It a Gift?

Here I think it is very important to ask ourselves, "What is the beginning assumption that we have about existence?" Part of what causes us to interpret as we do, lies in whether or not we see our life in history as *something to which we are entitled;* or whether we see it as a *gracious gift,* something that comes to us beyond our deserving, something that simply breaks in on our lives like a windfall?

I believe that the way you begin your thinking about your existence, your basic assumption, is really the *clue* as to why you interpret as you do. Those who have *a spirit of entitlement* are going to look at life one way. Those who see existence as *an undeserved gift* are going to interpret it differently. Maybe I can make clear what I mean by the "spirit of entitlement vs. the spirit of gracious gift" if I tell you of two trips I took, widely separated in years, very different in circumstances, and very different in terms of the spirit of interpretation that each of them evoked from me.

In 1975 my wife, Lue Ann, and I went to a Baptist World Alliance gathering in Stockholm, Sweden. We had been warned ahead of time that the prices in Scandinavia were astronomical, but not even the warnings prepared me for what it really was going to cost. We checked into a middle-range hotel in Stockholm and to my amazement, I discovered that I was going to be charged the equivalent of 200 American dollars a night. (That was in 1975!) Maybe some of you "high-rollers" are used to spending that kind of money. But I have never in all my life paid that much for a room. I was overcome and a little angry. When we went up to the room for which that exorbitant charge was being made, believe me I was looking at every detail with a very critical eye. The first thing I noticed was that there was only one set of towels, and I was on the "horn" in a matter of minutes, calling down to the desk, "For $200 a day at least we both ought to be able to dry off. You get some towels up here as quickly as possible!"

When the air conditioner didn't work, I complained. That whole week was spent with my being hypercritical about that room because the exorbitant price gave me a heightened sense of *entitlement.* If I were going to pay that much money, then I was going to be critical about the details of what was being given.

**What a Contrast!**

Take that experience in Stockholm and let me contrast it with something that happened many years before, in fact, back in 1947 when I was a senior in high school in Nashville, Tennessee. Somebody in our school decided it would be nice if the officers of the student government could go that year to the Southern Association of Student Governments meeting in Corpus Christi, Texas. Nobody from our high school had ever done that before.

The Father's Club gave a spaghetti dinner. Lots of people sacrificially chipped in. And enough money was finally gathered together to send three of us who were officers and our teacher-sponsor. In order to conserve our money, we took the train, not the pullman, mind you. We rode the day coach for 18 straight hours from Tennessee through Arkansas, all across Texas—18 hours sitting up in order to get to our destination. We couldn't afford to stay in a hotel. We had arranged to stay in a private home in Corpus Christi. When we got there, these lovely people said, "We only have two rooms we can give you. You two boys will have to sleep in the same bed, and your teacher and the girl with you may occupy the other room."

There was only one bathroom to take care of all of us. We lived rather far from town, but they said they had an old car that used to belong to their grandmother. It was old but dependable. They said we could use it if we wanted to. So we went back and forth to the convention all in a 1937 Ford that I sometimes wondered if it were going to make it.

The point I am making is that all the details of the Corpus Christi trip were very, very meager, but I don't remember having one resentful thought, for the simple reason that I had never expected to make that trip. It was a gift that had simply been given me from beyond. It was a windfall. Nobody from our high school had ever done anything like that. Therefore I was very, very grateful. I was not critical at all of the details because at the beginning, my assumption was that here was something I am being given, not because I deserve it, but because another is being generous. And when I set the attitude of Corpus Christi over against the attitude of Stockholm—do you see what I mean? When there is *a spirit of entitlement* it tends to heighten our resentment, to make us hypercritical. But when there is a *sense of "giftedness,"* a sense of graciousness, that gives us a very different perspective. And the way we interpret the details of a given situation is going to be vastly affected in terms of whether or not we think it is ours by *right* or whether we know it to be ours by *gift.*

## Life: A Gracious Gift

It seems to me that if we can ever realize that our very existence in history, our bodies, our chance to live, everything about our lives, is not something that we deserve; it is not something that we have earned our way into, but rather that the very way of being, the very essence of life is rightly understood as a *gracious gift,* that it comes to us from He who did not have to create us, but who wanted to create us; who did not need us in the sense that He had to have our existence, but rather wanted to share with us the joy of His aliveness.

If it ever begins to dawn on me that life is a *gift,* that God has given me my chance to *be* because He wants me to get in on His kind of joy, then that sense of *life as a gift,* over against the idea that I am *entitled* to it, is going to do two things for me. It is going to enable me to make the most of the positive things that I have been given, and it is going to enable me to make the best of the less-than-perfect circumstances that make up the terrain of all of our lives.

If I ever realize that life itself is a gift, undeserved, that it comes to me because of the generosity of another, and not because of my own efforts, then it makes me very, very grateful for the people and the things I have. It keeps me from being bitter and resentful and clinging. It opens me to live compassionately and gratefully with all the circumstances of my life.

## A Beautiful Story

Let me share a beautiful story with you about what it is like to feel life is a gift and be able to look at a very terrible trauma in a most positive way. It is found in the journal of a man named Hugh Prather. He had only been married a few years when his wife became seriously ill. He was not at all sure she was going to live through the night because she was critically—very critically—ill. As he sat by her bed in the hospital in those long, dark, quiet hours, these are the words that he wrote in his journal:

"She may die before morning but I have been with her for four years. There is no way I could feel cheated if I didn't have her for another day. God knows I didn't deserve her for a single moment. And *I* might die before morning. What I must do is accept the justice of death and the injustice of life. I have lived a good life, longer than many, better than most. Tony died when he was 20. I have had 32 years. I couldn't ask for another day. After all, what did I do to deserve birth? It was a gift, and I am "me." That is a miracle. I have no right to a single minute. Some are given but a single hour. Yet I have been given 32 years. Few can choose when they will die. I choose to accept death now. As of this moment, I give up my right to life and I give up my right to her life. But wait—it's morning! I am being given another day—another day to hear, and read, and smell, and walk in love and glory. I am alive for another day. And it's a gift!"

That's what it means to interpret existence from the vantage point that what I am—the very essence of my chance to be alive in history—is something that comes to me from somewhere else—not a spirit of entitlement which makes me hypercritical of all of my details, but this incredible wonder that I have been given life. I have the chance to be alive because God wants to give it to me. And that sense of life as a gift enables us to make the most of the positive things that we have been given, to be grateful for that which has come out of grace into our lives, not to cling to people as if they were our possessions. But like Prather, in relation to his wife, to hold people gently in hands of gratitude, to wonder and revel in the fact that we have had them, like snowflakes, even for a single day. And even if we are called on to give them up— if we realize that life is a gift—then, instead of being angry that they have been taken away, we have occasion to be grateful that they were ever given at all!

## Choosing To Be Bitter or Grateful

The difference between looking on a scene and being bitter—and looking on a scene and being grateful—the difference depends on your beginning assumption: is life an entitlement or is it an incredible gift?

I have said that life as gift enables us to make the most of the things we have going for us. It also enables us to make the best of the less-than-perfect circumstances that we all have to face. I remember a number of years ago hearing Carlyle Marney tell that when he was a pastor in Austin, Texas, there was born into his church family a perfect little girl except for one thing—she had no arms or legs. Except for that she had a perfect physique. This child happened to be born into a family that had several other children. They had a good bit of financial resource. So they decided to take this child who was tragically deformed, and instead of putting her into an institution, they would care for her at home and give her all the advantages that they could. They surrounded her with love. They gave her every compensatory skill they knew how, and according to Marney, she grew into a delightful spirit.

It turns out that she had a fantastic mind. She quickly learned to read. They gave her all kinds of educational opportunities, and she became a delight to all who came in contact with her.

When she was twenty years old, her brother who was in college, brought home a roommate for the weekend. I need to tell you he was a philosophy major. You know what a philosophy major is. He is the man who has these deep furrows in his brow. He is taking life terribly, terribly seriously. He is the kind of person who, if you met him on the campus, instead of saying, "How are you?" says, "Why are you?" He is really into getting to the analytic bottom of everything.

Well, this young sophomore philosopher saw this human

being in full shape except having no arms and no legs, having never been able to move herself a single inch, never able to feed herself, never able to do so many things that most of us take for granted. He was there for three days and saw her tragic deformity. On leaving he said to her, "I don't see what keeps you from being so angry at whatever kind of God allowed you to be born this way. Why don't you shake your fist in God's face and tell Him you are so angry about the terrible injustice that has been done to you?"

Marney tells that the girl heard him out, and then said very, very directly, "I realize, when compared to what other people have, what I have seems to be very, very little. But listen, friend, I wouldn't have missed the chance to be alive for anything. I have been able to see, and to hear, and to taste. I have gotten to know the splendors of the world, and to read the great things of the mind. I wouldn't have missed the chance to be alive for anything!"

**The Courage to Cope**

I want to suggest to you that the courage to cope with those kinds of desperately difficult circumstances comes, I think, from the vantage point of seeing life as "gift" rather than "entitlement."

You remember that Prather talked about the justice of death and the injustices of life. If you recognize the graciousness (e.g. the basic characteristic of existence), that we are given things not because we deserve them but because God wants to bequeath them to us. Then when you talk about injustice, the great injustice is the grace of existence itself.

And once you realize you are here not because you deserve it but because you have been given a chance to live by a gracious God, then you are able to make the best of the things of your life, the things that have all kinds of difficult challenges built into them. Then you can take the hard cards that are dealt to everyone of us in the course of our lives, and instead of being bitter and resentful, saying, "It's not fair. I don't deserve that," there is this tremendous resilience that says, "I wouldn't have missed the chance to be alive for anything. I am willing to pick up the hand that life has dealt to me. I am determined to make the best of the circumstances, the best of the worst, and the most of the best."

The courage to cope, the courage to look through the bars, where everyone of us has some mud to look at but also some stars. That which makes us either look down or up, I am confident, is whether or not as a beginning point we see life as a *gift* or as an *entitlement.*

### God Did Not *Have* to Create Us!

What it seems like to me is that the Christian gospel—with the perspective that it gives to every one of our lives—reminds us that life is a gift, that God did not *have* to create us. There is nothing in the Genesis account that indicates that a gun was put to His head and that He was forced to create out of some kind of external coercion that magnificent "Let there be. . . let there be. . . let there be. . . " that is the resonance of the whole first chapter of Genesis. This indicated to me that creation is, at bottom, an act of generosity. God felt His own aliveness to be so overwhelmingly wonderful that He said this is too good to keep, I want others to get in on the ecstasy that I am experiencing, so He decided to create, not in order to get something for Himself, but to *give* something of Himself.

And to sense that your life, my life, whatever chance of existence we have is, at bottom, a gracious gift. It seems to me that that attitude is the key to making grateful use of the good things we have and courageous use of the circumstances and challenges that are ours.

**Overwhelming News**

Gettis MacGregor, who teaches philosophy out in California, tells that when he was about five years old, he went with his mother to see his grandmother on a family vacation. The two ladies were sitting on the porch one day talking, as families do when they relax together. Not knowing that little Gettis was anywhere around, the grandmother said to the mother, "I am so glad that you decided to go ahead and have little Gettis because he has been such a joy to us all."

As you might guess, little Gettis *was* around, and when those words were said, his ears picked up and he bounded up on the porch. He wanted to know what his grandmother meant. Then he learned something about his early beginnings that he had never known. His mother had been 48 when she conceived him. She had read all the reports about how the older the mother the greater the problems with pregnancy. There had been considerable discussion with the doctor as to whether they should risk this late-life pregnancy. Finally at the last minute they decided to go ahead and do it. And that's what the grandmother meant, "I am so glad you decided to go ahead and have little Gettis." This was news to him—that there had been discussion about his coming into the world. He said he went off by himself with this new piece of information, and as a result had two overwhelming experiences.

The first was envisioning himself standing in a line moving slowly to a great portal over which was written the word *birth*. And just before he got to the door, a hand reached out, pulled him from the line, and a voice said, "You have been disqualified." The horror of never having been born washed over him with all of its power.

Then after that a second impression came: he had gotten through the door. For all the discussion that had gone on, he had in fact been given the gift of life and was allowed to be born. MacGregor says that from five years of age on he never took for granted that his life had been given to him. He got up every morning, remembering that he might not have been, and therefore savored with wonder the fact that he was.

*You* can do the same thing. Your being born was a gracious gift of God, not something that you earned but something that He gave you. The sense of *life as a gift* is the essence of gratitude and courage.

"Two men looked through the self-same bars. One saw mud, the other stars." The stargazer did what he did because he realized that *life is a gift.* It is that for us all. Hallelujah!

*Peter Kreeft's books occupy a special place in my library, as they do in many others. This award-winning Boston College professor writes at a spiritual depth few others attain.*

# The One Thing We Can't Live Without

## Peter J. Kreeft

How can I know that God loves me? I believe it, or I want to. But how can I know it for sure? How can I get assurance of the most important thing in the world?

The question is an excellent one. It demands something more than the mere mental acceptance of the three-word proposition "God loves me." It demands three greater forms of intimacy or closeness.

*First,* I want to know that God loves *me,* not just everyone. Me, with all my very specific and very real sins and uglinesses and unloveablenesses. Does God really love me just as I am? Am I really completely forgiven?

*Second, I* need to know that God loves me. I need not just general assurance but individual, personal assurance. "It's in the Bible" or even "Jesus said so" is not enough. Though that makes it *true,* it has to become also *true for me* in the proper sense of that much misused term: I must interiorize this objective truth. I must have what Cardinal

John Henry Newman called "real assent," not just "notional assent."

I can indeed know that God loves me in the same way that you or anyone else can: God said so. There are objective facts. There is data. Christianity is a religion of facts, not just values. It appeals to a public, objective revelation, not just subjective and private mystical experiences and subtle insights. I can know God loves me by looking at Christ in the Gospels.

But I also need the individual, interior conversion of mind, the correction of will, and the conviction of heart. I need to personally appropriate this objective truth. Christ tells the world who God is. The Holy Spirit tells me. Christ is the public Word of God, the Spirit is the private Word. Christ promises that "He (The Holy Spirit) will take what is Mine and declare it to you" (John 16:14). Both are necessary.

*Third,* I need to *know* that God loves me. It must be a certainty, not an opinion, and more than belief. Belief is not even in the same league with knowing. It's not even playing the same game. And opinion is the weakest kind of knowledge, for it is guaranteed by the One who can neither deceive nor be deceived.

I need such a guarantee if I am to rest all my eggs in the one strange basket that God offers me. For if it isn't true, all is lost. "Christian faith," says T.S. Elliot, "is a condition of complete simplicity / Costing not less than / Everything." If my faith is false, the whole meaning of my life and death is gone. Faith is not an ingredient in my life. It must be the foundation that holds up all the other stories of my life. I need an absolutely sure foundation.

And in the words of the old hymn by Samuel Stone, "The Church's one foundation is Jesus Christ her Lord," Jesus is the proof that God loves me. And His Spirit will give me absolute personal certainty if I ask Him, just as He did to the disciples, just as Jesus promised He would for all who ask (Luke 11:9-13).

## But What About Suffering

The most common and apparently the strongest argument against faith in the God of love is suffering. More people have turned sour on God because of that than anything else. If God is love, why do bad things happen to good people?

Once again, Christ is the answer as the love of God made visible. Christ transforms the meaning and value of suffering from something to be endured into something that is redemptive. His suffering changes the meaning of suffering and thus of our suffering, just as His death changes the meaning of death and thus of our death. Our suffering can be grafted into the very sufferings of Christ (Col. 1:24).

God's answer to the problem of suffering was to carry it Himself: "Surely He has borne our griefs and carried our sorrows" (Isa. 53:4). Far from disproving God's love, suffering draws that love down into itself like a magnet on Calvary.

But Calvary's spectacular solution to the strongest of all objections against God's love presupposes that Christ is God, not just another good man who was defeated at the end. Only if He is God can His sufferings be universally effective for all and for me.

My suffering unites me with God partly because it dissolves the glue that bonds me to the one thing that keeps me from God: my own self-will. This is the "I want what I want when I want it" principle that theologians call original sin. Suffering conforms me more closely to the likeness of the One who called not His own will His own, but welcomed every opportunity to say, "Not my will but thine be done." Saints embrace suffering for one reason only: the love of God.

In a universe ruled by an all-loving and all-powerful God, no suffering can be wasted. The answer to the question, "Can it do anyone any good?" has to be "Yes."

It may do others good rather than myself when I suffer, for we are all one family, one body, and we suffer for each other. But this means it is for me, too, for I am part of this body. What I give, I also receive. If my suffering contributes to the greater health and strength of the body of Christ, then I also *receive* that greater health and strength if I am in that body.

Sufferings don't *automatically* do anyone any good. They must be willed, accepted, believed, offered up, and joined to Christ's. Much suffering can be wasted and is. But *any* suffering *can* do someone good. God would not allow it otherwise.

What, finally, should we do about suffering if we love God and know that He loves us? What is the practical formula? Simply to use it, as everything else is used, for the end we know is the end of all things: God's love getting its way. Augustine's formula is simple and perfect. Only God is to be loved for His own sake. Everything else is to be loved for God's sake. God is to be loved and things are to be used. God is the final end, and things are the means. People are ends, too, because they are not things but images of God. But they are not our final end.

### We Need to Recover the Awe of God's Love

The disappearance of the experience of awe, worship, wonder, and holy fear is the single most radical psychological loss in modern times. The most blasphemous form of this loss, I think, is the trivialization of the love of God to something like candy, even cotton candy, something ineffably *nice*, something *comfortable*.

Thinking of the love of God as something nice is forgetting that the love of God is the love *of God*. The awesomeness of God makes the love of God equally awesome. As Rabbi Abraham Heschel, the great Jewish theologian of the twentieth century, said, "God is not nice.

God is not an uncle. God is an earthquake." If you do not like that (one of my students responded to that quotation with, "I prefer a God I can handle." Indeed!), then you do not like the love of God, for the love of God is also an earthquake, not an uncle's love, but a Father's.

There is no greater earthquake. It is the "still, small voice" that is greater than the physical earthquake or the fire or the hurricane (I Kings 19:9-13). This is the earthquake that turned the world upside down (Acts 17:6), turned the sun to darkness and darkness to light on Calvary, ripped the veil of the Holy of Holies in the Temple, and shattered the insulation between earth and heaven. If understanding the significance of the greatest event that ever happened will not restore awe, nothing will.

### God's Love is Our Only Anchor

We live in an age of troubled morals everywhere, of infidelities in the board room and the bedroom, of scandals in high places and low places, of greed and corruption in politics and the courts, of revelations of lusts and lies and cheating in the pulpits. Whom can we trust anymore?

We live in the age of "anything goes," the age of "everyone does it," the Age of Kinsey where half of all marriages end in divorce and three-fourths of those who stay married harbor regrets and second thoughts.

Divorce is a sin not only (1) against God and his law, (2) against your partner, (3) against the truth (for you solemnly swore fidelity till death) and thus against yourself and your honesty, but (4), most tragically it is a sin against the innocent and vulnerable ones, the children. Rip away all the polite but cruel coverups. The truth is that *divorce is always* devastating to the kids; and everybody knows it, even those who try to rationalize it. If it is not devastating to the kids, that means they're cynical enough to accept it. That's even more devastating. Divorce is parental infidelity. When you can't even trust your own mother and father, whom can you trust?

"When my father and mother forsake me, then the Lord will take me up" (Psalm 27:10, KJV). Is that pious rhetoric? No, it is absolutely essential psychological anchoring in a world where there are no other absolutely trustworthy anchors, a world where your own parents or your own spouse may one day let you down. (How do you know they won't? No one who has been betrayed ever expected to be.) In a world of universal moral failure, only God will never fail you; and if you don't know that, you will go quietly insane.

If God is not absolute love, we are doomed. If Christ on the cross is not something more than just another good man betrayed, if Christ is not God incarnate, definitely revealing the truth of God's never-give-up, go-all-the-way love—then let's all just quietly pack it up and go home. (But without God, we have no home!)

There are ultimately only two possibilities: God's Love, or despair. That's why God's love is the one thing we can't live without.

*Although Henry Drummond lived only 28 years, this young Scot made a profound impact on the religious and scientific world of the late 19th century—an impact that is still with us today. His books outsold all the popular novels of his time, and he assisted Dwight L. Moody in evangelistic campaigns in England, Scotland and Ireland.*

# The Greatest Thing in the World

## Henry Drummond

L ove is like light. As you have seen a man of science take a beam of light and pass it through a crystal prism, you will see it come out on the other side broken up into its component colors: red, blue, yellow, violet, orange, and all the colors of the rainbow. In the universally loved 13th chapter of I Corinthians, Paul passes this thing, love, through the magnificent prism of his inspired intellect, and it comes out on the other side broken up into its elements.

I Corinthians 13:4-6 lists the nine ingredients of love:

Patience ... "Love suffereth long."

For love understands, and therefore waits.

Kindness ... "And is kind."

Kindness is love in action. I wonder why it is that we are not all kinder than we are. How the world needs it! How easily it is done! How instantaneously is acts! How infallibly it is remembered!

145

Generosity . . . "Love envieth not."

> Whenever you attempt a good work you will find others doing the same kind of work, and probably doing it better. Envy them not. Envy is a spirit of ill-will, covetousness, and detraction.

Humility . . . "Love vaunteth not itself, is not puffed up."

> After you have been kind, after love has stolen forth into the world and done its beautiful things, go back into the shade again and say nothing about it. Love hides even from itself.

Courtesy . . . "Doth not behave itself unseemly."

> This is love in society, love in relation to etiquette. Love cannot behave itself unseemly . . . You know the meaning of the word, "gentleman." It means a *gentle* man—a man who does things gently, with love. (Of course, the same goes for "ladies.")

Unselfishness . . . "Love seeketh not her own."

> The most obvious lesson in Christ's teaching is that there is no happiness in having or in getting anything,—only in giving. He that would be happy, let him remember there is but one way. "It is more blessed, it is more happy, to give than to receive."

Good temper . . . "Love is not easily provoked."

> For embittering life, for breaking up communities, for destroying the most sacred relationships, for devastating homes, for withering up men and women, for taking the bloom off of childhood, in short, for sheer gratuitous misery-producing power, this influence stands alone. It is not in what temper is alone, but in what it reveals. Hence we must go to the source and allow Christ to change the inmost nature. Souls are made sweet not by taking the acid fluids out but by putting in a great love, a new spirit, the Spirit of Christ.

That is what sweetens, purifies, and transforms all.

Guilelessness . . . "Taketh not account of evil."

Love sees the bright side, puts the best construction on every action. What a delightful state of mind to live in! What a stimulus and benediction even to meet with it for a day!

Sincerity . . . "Does not rejoice at wrong, but rejoices in the right."

Love refuses to make capital out of others' faults. It is the charity which delights not in exposing the weakness of others, rather the sincerity of purpose that endeavors to see things as they are and rejoices to find them better than suspicion feared.

So much for the analysis of love. Now the business of our lives is to have these things fitted into our characters. That is the supreme work to which we need to address ourselves—to learn to love. Is life not full of opportunities for learning love? The world is not a playground; it is a schoolroom. Life is not a holiday, but an education. And the eternal lesson for all of us is how better we can love.

**Learning to Love**

What makes a good artist, a good sculptor? Practice. What makes a good linguist? A good stenographer? Practice. What makes a person a good person? Practice. Love is not a thing of enthusiastic emotion. It is a rich, strong vigorous expression of the whole round Christian character—the Christ-like nature in its fullest development. And the constituents of this great character are only to be built up by ceaseless practice.

Do not resist the hand that is molding the still shapeless image within you. It is growing more beautiful, though you see it not; and every touch of temptation may add to its perfection. Therefore, keep in the midst of life. Do not isolate yourself. Be among people and among things, and among troubles and difficulties and obstacles. Remember Goethe's words: "Talent develops itself in solitude; character in the stream of life." The talent of prayer, of faith, of meditation of seeing the unseen, develop in solitude; character grows in the stream of the world's life. That is where we are to learn love.

### What Causes Love?

In I John 4:19, you will read, "We love because He first loved us." Look at the word "because." It is because He loves us that we can love. Contemplate the love of Christ, and you will love. Stand before that mirror, reflect Christ's character, and you will be changed into the same image from tenderness to tenderness. There is no other way. You cannot love to order. You can only look at the lovely object, and fall in love with it, and grow into its likeness.

It is the love of God that melts down our unlovely hearts and begets a new creature in us—one that is patient and humble and gentle and unselfish. There is no other way to get it. There is no mystery about it. We love others, we love everybody, we love even our enemies, because He first loved us.

### Love Lasts! It Never Fails!

Paul's reason for singling out love as the supreme possession is a remarkable one. It lasts! "Love," urges Paul, "never fails." Then he begins again one of his marvelous lists of the great things of the day, and exposes them one by one. He runs over the things that men thought were going to last, and shows that they are all fleeting, temporary, passing away.

Can you tell me anything that is going to last? Many things Paul did not condescend to name. He did not mention money, fortune, fame; but he picked out the great things of his time, the things the best men thought had something in them, and brushed them aside. Paul had nothing against these things in themselves. All he said about them was that they would not last. They were great things, but not supreme things. There were things beyond them. What we are stretches past what we do, beyond what we possess.

## To Love Abundantly is to Live Abundantly

To love abundantly is to live abundantly, and to love forever is to live forever. Hence, eternal life is inextricably bound up with love. We want to live forever for the same reason we want to live tomorrow. Why do we want to live tomorrow? Is it because there is someone who loves us, and whom we want to see tomorrow, and be with, and love back? There is no other reason why we should live than that we love and be loved. It is when people have no one to love that they commit suicide. So long as we have friends, those who love us and whom we love, we will live, because to live is to love. Be it but the love of a dog, love will keep us in life; but let that go, and we have no contact with life, no reason to live, and we choose to die.

How many of you will join me in reading the 13th chapter of I Corinthians once a week for the next three months? A man did that once, and it changed his whole life! Will you do it? You might begin by reading it every day, especially the verses that describe the perfect character, "Love suffereth long, and is kind; love envieth not; love vaunteth not itself." Get these ingredients into your life. Then everything you do is eternal. It is worth giving time to. No one can become a saint in his sleep; and to fulfill the condition required demands a certain amount of prayer and meditation and time, just as improvement, bodily or mental, requires preparation and practice.

You will find as you look back on your life the moments that stand out, the moments when you have really lived, are the moments when you have done things in a spirit of love. As memory scans the past, above and beyond all the transitory pleasures of life, there leap forward those supreme hours when you have been enabled to do some unnoticed kindnesses to those around you, things too trifling to speak about. The acts of love which no one knows about, or can ever know about are the ones that will remain.

Thank God the Christianity of today is coming nearer to the world's need. Thank God we know better, by a hair's breadth, what God is, who Christ, is, where Christ is. Who is Christ? He who fed the hungry, clothed the naked, visited the sick. And where is Christ? Where? "Whoso shall receive a little child in my name receiveth me." And who are Christ's? "Everyone who loves is born of God." Love. The greatest thing in the world is love!

*Ann Kiemel Anderson is a best-selling author of numerous books and winner of the C. S. Lewis Award. One of her first books,* I'm Out to Change My World, *is considered a classic, and I know you will enjoy this excerpt.*

# You Just Can't Stop Love!

## Ann Kiemel Anderson

You just can't stop love.
It crushes barriers.
It breaks and builds bridges
It finds a way through.
It never gives up.
It's hard work.
It listens.
It walks ten miles.
It's something you do.
Jesus did it for me.
He died to set me free.
He lives to share my life with me.
and I go to His
and
my people
and love wins.

One kid,
  his name was John,
    walked around with his head down all the time.
He never looked you in the eye,
  And if you ever got close to him,
    he shuddered.
  One day John wasn't there
    and I said to the kids,
  "Let's try an experiment.
    Let's really love John.
  I mean,
    really love him
  As we've never loved anyone before.
    Let's see what love can do for John."
He was the most inhibited, insecure kid
  I had ever seen in my life.
    From that moment on we asked Jesus
      to help us love John.
We sent him letters.
  We wrote notes during the week.
    We stopped by to buy him a coke.
After six months of loving John,
  the kids started to get tired.
"Gee, Ann,
  you don't know what its like to love John.
We call him at home
  to see how his week is going,
and he says, 'M-m-m, OK.'
  "John," you say,
"I really have been thinking of you
  and I love you,"
    and he just grunts.

But I'll never forget the morning
  we were all gathered together
    and suddenly

John smiled.
We had never seen John smile.
He really smiled.
And two weeks later when he laughed out loud,
it nearly blew our minds!
No one wanted John to notice, but they
were all trying to signal me—
"Had I noticed?"
John laughed,
he really laughed.


Three weeks later
his mother, who was a non-Christian—
the whole family was non-Christian—
called me and said,
"Ann,
last weekend we were in the mountains camping.
John is 16
and I haven't seen him cry since he was five.
But he started to cry and bawl and sob.
and after four hours
I was almost frantic.
I asked him why he was crying like this.
All he could say over and over was,
'I'm such a failure, Mom,
I'm such a flop.'

And finally I said,
'It's that church you're going to,
they're not treating you right.'
And he said as he shook his head,
'No, no.
It's my only hope, Mom.
They love me over there.' "

And she said,
   "It seemed like the minute he said that,
the minute he came out and shared that with me,
   he began to dry his tears,
      and he straightened his back
   and held his head up.
And it's strange,
   he's never been the same since.

And in the group
   he began to laugh a lot.
He began to share in conversational prayer
   when we prayed.
He began to bring a friend on Sunday,
   and two friends the next Sunday
and he became the best softball player we ever had.
   For the first time in his life
      he had the courage to play ball.

*Love* changed John's life,
   *just love*
You can do one of two things in your world.
   You can build a wall
      or you can build a bridge
      to every person you meet.

               I'm out to build bridges,
                  Are you?
            Come and build bridges with me.
                  Sir,
               can I take your hand?
                  or yours ma'am?
            Can I pick you up little boy
               and hold you in my lap
               and kiss your cold face
                  even if it's dirty?

Can I love you to Him?
Can I love you so much
through thick and thin
until you learn
that Jesus really cares for you?
Can I love you until you feel hope for the world
and your tomorrows?
That's my hope.

That's my story.
And it can be yours.

*During the 28 years he served as pastor of the Pleasant Ridge Presbyterian Church in Cincinnati (of which he is now pastor Emeritus), Clyde York preached many memorable sermons, one of which won the George Washington Memorial Award for "Best Sermon of the Year."*

# Pass It On

## Clyde O. York

**M**any years ago, when I was still a young man, I came upon an older man who was planting a tree in his front yard. Charlie straightened up as I approached and pushed at the small of his back as if to get some strained parts back in place. "I'll bet you're wondering why I'm doing this, aren't you?" he asked.

Before I had a chance to answer, he continued. "I know as old as I am that I'll never see this tree amount to much. It'll never make enough shade to do *me* any good. It's for Caroline." He was referring to the 12-year-old girl who was his only grandchild. "Someday Caroline will enjoy this tree."

Charlie died some 15 years later, and Caroline—as well as others—did sit under the shade of the tree. Many people reaped the blessing of another man's caring.

### Most of Us Sit Under Trees We Didn't Plant

Most of us sit under trees that we did not plant. Conscience tells us that, in turn, we ought to plant a tree

156

for some generation yet to come. A middle-aged man without a family complained one day about the system of taxes. "It's not fair," he said, "I pay hundreds of dollars in school taxes, yet no child of mine has ever used this school system." "Wait a minute," a wise man interrupted, "You aren't paying for the schooling these kids are getting. You're paying for the education you were given thirty years ago. You're a little late, but don't feel bad about it. All of us are."

That's the way it is with our human story. We have inherited so much—trees others have planted, schools, libraries and churches others have built, inventions and discoveries others have developed, freedoms others have won. There is no way to pay those who have made such benefits available to us, but we can pass them on. We opened our hands at birth and found others generations pouring abundance upon us. Somehow, in the course of life, we must pass on what we have received, and by the grace of God, a little more than we received.

## The Most Difficult to Pass On

Now of all the things you have received, the most important is also the most difficult to pass on. Past generations with their more open expressions of piety would sometimes include in their last will and testament a sentence, something like this—"And to my children I bequeath a living faith in God, and a dedication to those holy principles which undergird human life and character." When you read such a document, you only wish it were possible to pass along faith, honor, and character, as simply as you bequeath a piece of land and shares of stock. The best things in life are free, as the lyricist has said, but they are also the most difficult to pass on to another generation.

The fact is, nearly all the best things in life are always just one generation from extinction. A good deal is said these days, and rightly, about those rare species which are vanishing from the world of nature. But among our endangered species, none is more fragile than the quality of life presented to us in the Scriptures of the Old and New Testaments. Human freedom, a sense of respect for human life, love, the rights of the individual and the rights of society—all these are in peril in every generation, and especially so in ours.

Moses, the greatest of all law-givers, understood this. By God's help, he had taken a nation of oppressed slaves and had led them to freedom. They had been a subject people for several generations. Not one of them could remember what freedom was like. Not one, with the exception of Moses, had known what it was to be treated with dignity and respect. But God laid bare His arm and opened a highway for them through the sea, and then watched over them in the wilderness.

But what about the next generation? How would they know the value of freedom, and how would they understand the faithfulness of God? Moses knew that if this priceless love of God and freedom were not passed on to the next generation, the Jewish people would soon lose everything that mattered. So he gave the people a number of religious ceremonies, saying, "And when in time to come your son asks you—what does this mean—you shall say to him, by strength of hand, the Lord brought us out of Egypt from the house of bondage." Pass it on . . . Tell your children that they may tell their children, that there shall never be a generation without the knowledge of God's mighty goodness."

Dr. Brevard Childs, points out that the tradition was not only to be passed on to subsequent generations, but that it was to be experienced. It was something to be in their mouths, written on their hands, carried as a frontlet between their eyes. Later generations of Jews interpreted the command literally, making items to be worn on the body which would remind them of their tie with God and His law. They considered the religious education of their children to be one of the most important of the divine commands. For unless faith was passed along from parent to child, from old to young, it would surely inevitably die out.

### "Trust in God and Do Right"

Some generations have followed this command to the best of their ability, and their efforts bore results. Thomas Carlyle grew up in a little community in Southern Scotland where life was narrow and sheltered. In his years of international acclaim, he might so easily have lost his moorings. He insisted that what kept him right was his mother's voice across the years in a saying she had impressed deep in his soul. "Trust in God and do right." How fortunate to have such counsel echoing in one's soul.

In the same way it is significant that Jesus, in the hour of His death on Calvary, spoke the prayer, "Father, into Thy hands I commit my spirit." That sentence, except for the word Father, which Jesus added, was the first goodnight prayer every Jewish mother in ancient Israel taught her child to say before going to sleep. Of all the prayers Jesus might have spoken in the hour of dying, He chose the one which had first been given to Him in His childhood home. When life is at a crisis, we try to plumb down to bedrock. How good when some parent, or teacher or minister has given us such a foundation; and how tragic if we reach down for a solid base, and there is nothing there.

But some in our generation are reluctant to influence the young. We have passed through a period in which youth has been idealized. It was a strange irrational mood. Many adults were so impressed with the potential of youth, that they completely forgot the value of experience. One could only conclude, in listening to those who are abdicating their adult responsibility that if we know less at 45 than we know at 17, it would be better for everyone to be destroyed at 18 or 20 before we begin to deteriorate. The hope of the future is, indeed, in the child. But a child will not get right concepts by magic, or by wondrous chance. There must be someone who will pass along to the next generation the best of what the *previous* generations have learned.

### Choice is Never Made in a Vacuum

But one of you interjects, "The new generation should be free to choose for itself." Well they should. But their choice is never made in a vacuum. If parents and teachers and ministers do not make an impression for goodness, you can be sure that someone will make an impression for what is evil and base. If a child is not stimulated to love what is good, someone, somewhere, will try to win him for evil. Our world has many who will make a case for hate and cheating, who will try to hook a child on drugs, who will try to cultivate an appetite for what is shoddy. The person who lives with lying and deception, the one who wallows in smut and cheapness is always trying to get someone to join him. And when people excuse their conduct by saying everybody's doing it, they are trying to guarantee that such will be the case. For they are made uneasy by those who set a higher standard. Let no one assume that young persons will choose simply from the inspiration of their own pure spirit. They will choose on the basis of the case they have heard; and if no one makes a strong, attractive case for God and for goodness, we should not be surprised that they choose a poorer way.

We have a descriptive phrase in American speech. We speak of "Shirtsleeves to shirtsleeves in three generations." That is, some industrious man of moderate circumstances works his way from shirtsleeves to economic comfort. His children continue in that state but with some diminishing of energy. His grandchildren drop off still further, and his great-grandchildren are back in the shirtsleeves that the old man worked to leave behind. Let me adapt the insight to religious terms and say that it is often only three generations from pagan to pagan. And sometimes only two. A secular sinful soul finds God and moves into purity and quality of life. His children follow his path, but perhaps not with the same ardor or depth of conviction. His grandchildren are only nominally religious, carrying their church membership card in the same wallet with their other social conveniences. And the third generation becomes afflicted with the very paganism from which that ancestor was once delivered.

### We Cannot "Pass On" What We Do Not Have

Well believe me, it is not an easy thing to pass on faith. One wishes it were a recipe like a favorite casserole that a mother gives to her daughter; or a laboratory formula which a scientist passes on to a new generation of chemists and physicists. But convictions and beliefs are not so easily passed along. The father may say, "Love the Lord your God witn all your heart, soul, mind and strength." But the son may hear, "Join the church." The parent may say, "Love the Lord your God with all your heart, soul, mind and strength." But the son may hear, "Mind your own business and keep out of trouble."

One thing is sure. We cannot pass on what we do not have. A new generation isn't likely to get a white-hot faith from their parents' lukewarm religion. One of the popular religious songs of this decade expresses the urgency and the joy of passing on the Good News in the phrase, "I want to pass it on." We can't jam our convictions down someone else's throat. If we do, the other person is likely to someday regurgitate them whole without ever having digested them. But we can say, "Here's what happened to me, and here is why I believe. You'll have to find it for yourself, for second-hand faith is never adequate. But I believe, and I'll tell you why I want to pass it on."

What I say here, I say not simply to mothers or to parents. They have a particularly heavy responsibility to pass along high values, and a unique power for doing so. But they are not alone. Teachers also have the calling—both secular teachers and Sunday School teachers. Ministers, of course, have such a responsibility. It is the very definition of their work. But brothers and sisters have it too. In many instances, a sibling can pass on faith and conviction to another in the family. Friends can do it. Some of the people who most enriched my life were friends of my parents' age and, later, friends of my own age.

## We Are Links in the Chain of Life

We are links in the chain of life. This world goes on because one generation passes the spark of life to another generation. Those qualities which make life worthwhile, including eternal life, are also passed on from one generation to another, and from one person to another. In the peculiar pressures of modern living, great values hang by a slender thread: kindliness and gentility, concern for others, a sense of personal worth, human freedom. But in most danger is that from which all the rest flows: faith in God and redemption through the cross of Christ.

All of us who have faith are enjoying shade from a tree someone else planted. If a good thing has come into your life, *pass it on.*

All of us who have faith are enjoying shade from trees planted by someone else. The following poem sums up the challenge that every generation must face:

## Hold High the Torch

Hold high the torch!
You did not light its glow.
Twas given you by others hands, you know.
Tis yours to keep it burning bright,
Yours to *pass on* when you no more need light;
For there are other feet that we must guide,
And other forms go marching by our side;
Their eyes are watching every smile and tear,
And efforts which we think are not worthwhile
Are sometimes just the very help they need,
Actions to which their souls would give most heed;
So that in turn, they will hold it high and say,
"I watched someone else carry it this way."
If brighter paths should beckon you to choose,
Would your small gain compare with all you'd lose?
Hold high the torch!
You did not light its glow.
Twas given you by others hands, you know.
I think it started down its pathway bright.
The day the Maker said, "Let there be Light!"
And He once said, who hung on Calvary's tree,
"You are the light of the world. Go, shine for Me."

—Author Unknown

# How To Make Sure You End Up A Winner

## Alice E. Flaherty

The day we brought him home, I had held him on my lap all the way, afraid he would break, I suppose. But when I lifted him out of the car and let him loose in the yard, what a transformation! He made a running circle of the yard, as if he wanted to make sure it was his— then, like a jack rabbit, he bounded up the walk to the front door. He couldn't wait for me to open it and let him inside.

That was Tiny Tim, our Schnauzer, returning home from the animal hospital where he had undergone a kidney operation. All of us, including his doctor, had been amazed that a dog his age (fourteen), could survive major surgery and recover so quickly. One thing was certain: there was one little guy who was happy to be home! Having a place to call home is crucially important, even to animals.

"I want to go home!" . . . "Take me home." . . . "I can't wait to get home." . . . Familiar phrases? To be sure. Home is that place we all want to get to at the end of a day's work, a tough day at school, or even after a wonderful vacation. And certainly, it is where we want to go when we are ill or discouraged about something. Remember when you were a child, playing with your friends? If something went wrong and everyone began to quarrel, somebody would invariably start to cry and "head for home." Yes, home is a haven, a shelter from the storms of life.

Christians look upon Heaven as their real home, and life in this world as primarily a journey that will lead them there. As believers, they know that no matter how rough things get here on earth, some day their loving Heavenly Father will welcome them Home, and all their earthly hurts will be forgotten.

I like what St. Paul wrote in his letter to the Ephesian Christians: "Now you are no longer strangers to God and foreigners to heaven . . . you are members of God's very own family, citizens of God's country, and you belong in God's household with every other Christian" (Eph. 2:19, TLB).

In a sense, we are cosmic orphans—born into this world with a subconscious desire to get back home to God. Dr. Maurice Rawlings, a specialist in cardiovascular diseases, writes in his excellent book, *Beyond Death's Door,* that our hope of immortality acts as a homing instinct, so deeply rooted that it has caused people to seek their Creator throughout the ages, perhaps just as homing instincts cause migrating birds, whales, and other animals to accurately seek their own refuge.

Peter Kreeft explains our built-in longing for God and immortality: we are all born with a God-shaped space in our heart that nothing else can fill. In *Heaven: The Heart's Deepest Longing,* he writes, "Everyone, not just religious people (whoever *they* are), is born, built, and designed to feed on God-food. And when we try to feed on other food, we starve."

Author Kreeft goes on to say, "There lives in us, deep down in the heart, a little nightingale that keeps calling for its birdseed. It is a bothersome but infinitely precious little bird. The nightingale lives way down under a host of larger, louder animals, each demanding its food; so it is easy to ignore. It has 'a still, small voice.' But when we ignore it, even if we feed all the other animals (which is impossible), we are not satisfied, because we *are* that nightingale, and we are starving."

The Bible assures us that God is aware of every sparrow's fall, that He calls all the stars by name, and that He has numbered the hairs of our heads. He knows the struggles and hardships that birds go through when they migrate and how hard the salmon have to work to swim upstream at spawning time. Think how much more He must be aware of how we struggle and stumble our way through life! And how it must grieve Him, when people refuse to accept His offer of eternal life with Him forever. Did you ever offer a gift to a person who turned away and wouldn't accept it? The Bible tells us how Jesus wept over Jerusalem—think how many tears He has shed over the world since then.

One of the last things He said on earth (before He ascended into Heaven), was that He was going to go to prepare a place for each of his own, so it would be ready when the time came for them to leave earth and go Home to Him. So when life gets to be too much, take comfort in the fact that this world is not all there is. Remember, it's only temporary, and that Heaven is your real Home.

### Heaven: God's Grand Prize

Show-dogs, devoted to their masters, seem to give outstanding performances when they are given praise and treats as rewards. Children, too, thrive when parents and teachers use the praise-and-reward system. Adults work toward goals and rewards in much the same way, a paycheck being the most basic. Then come the vacations and the things we buy or dream of doing someday, that make our lives more fulfilling and rewarding.

Prizes of all kinds hold a fascination for most everyone: from Olympic medals, or the honor of a Pulitzer Prize, to a blue ribbon for a handmade quilt or a jar of cucumber pickles at a country fair. People also strive to win in games of guesswork or pure chance; our society is being inundated with more and more ways and places to gamble. In the state lotteries, the bigger the jackpot, the more excited people become. Gambling casinos are increasing at an alarming rate. Others compete on television shows for expensive prizes and trips to exotic places, all with the hope of winning big! But sadly, many of those very same people will overlook the chance to go to Heaven and take part in the most glorious and exciting trip of all! And for that, no one has to gamble. It's a sure thing for those who honestly seek God and really *want* to accept His gift of salvation and eternal life. If I *were* forced to gamble on whether or not there is a Heaven, I would choose like the monk who took an atheist on a tour of his monastery. At the end, the atheist smugly said to the monk, "Just think now, if God doesn't exist, and I don't think He does, than you will have wasted your whole life." And the monk replied, "If I am wrong, I shall have wasted only some 70 years. But if *you* are wrong, you will have wasted an eternity!"

Christians don't look on heaven as a reward to be gambled on or earned by good works or a pleasant personality, but a reward for believing God and His promise to forgive their sins and save them for Heaven. That concept may sound a little strange to a person who is not yet a believer, for the world requires that we *earn* our rewards. But God's grand prize of everlasting life with Him cannot be earned like Brownie Points or Olympic medals; it is purely His gift of grace and love, and must be accepted on that basis.

The Apostle Paul understood this concept. He wrote, "I am still not all I should be, but I am bringing all my energies to bear on this one thing: Forgetting the past and looking forward to what lies ahead, I strain to reach the end of the race and receive the prize for which God is calling us up to Heaven because of what Christ did" (Phil. 3:13-14, TLB). Paul knew the prize that awaited him—not by his merits but because of what Christ did. Paul made no apology for looking forward to the joys of Heaven.

Even Jesus looked forward to the completion of His mission on earth. Scripture tells us that He was willing to die a shameful death on the Cross, because of the joy He knew would be His afterwards, and now He sits in the place of honor by the throne of God. And His joy would also include having all of His faithful followers with Him forever. In the last prayer Jesus prayed with His disciples, He said, "Father, I want them with Me—those you've given Me—so they can see My glory. . ." (John 17:24 TLB). Just think how He suffered in order for us to share in His Heavenly glory forever!

### What About Monday Morning

What does Heaven have to do with Monday morning? Everything! Practically all of life's decisions are made according to what we consciously or subconsciously believe about the future. Therefore, what we believe about eternity will greatly influence how we live, how much courage we can muster to meet our daily struggles, and whether life will hold a joy that is genuine and lasting.

The kind of joy I am talking about here is an unconquerable gladness that is rooted at the very core of our being. It is a supernatural joy that comes to us via God's "Amazing Grace" to support us in adversity, and hold us steady in success. Christians who have claimed this joy can do so, because they know who they are and where they are going.

It is because believers keep their relationship with God as their first priority that they can dare to love and live every day as it comes with courage and vigor. Yes, there *is* "a peace that passes understanding" (Phil. 4:7). As every seasoned Christian will tell you, "Make your peace with God through Christ first. Then, and only then, will you be ready to cope with life's struggles."

God has offered us a separate peace here on earth and a guaranteed happy ending in Heaven. So, it is really very simple to make sure you end up a winner. All you have to do is decide, once and for all, to say yes to God and His plan for your life.

If you are an unbeliever but are wishing you *could* believe, or if you are already a believer, but are caught in a valley of grief or disappointment, I suggest you take a Bible and go to some place where you can be alone, and "have it out" with God. Tell Him honestly how you feel, then stop talking and listen to what He has to say. Open the Bible to the Psalms. Slowly leaf through them and look for one that expresses how you feel (there are lots of them to pick from), and read it as a prayer. God will speak to your heart, as you read. I think you will be surprised at how much it helps.

Something else I would recommend to you, along with the Psalms, is the following quote from John Powell's *Fully Human, Fully Alive.* I have read it so often, I have it practically memorized.

> God says: I will be with you. I am covenanted, committed forever to love you; to do whatever is best for you. . . Remember your destiny is eternal life. God says: By all means join the dance and sing the songs of a full life. At the same time, remember that you are a pilgrim. you are on your way to an eternal home which I have prepared for you. Eternal life has already begun in you but it

is not perfectly completed. There are still inevitable sufferings. But remember that the sufferings of this present stage of your life are nothing compared to the glory that you will see revealed in you someday. . .

On your way to our eternal home, enjoy the journey. Let your happiness be double, in the joyful possession of what you have and in the eager anticipation of what will be. Say a resounding "Yes!" to life and to love at all times. Someday you will come up into my mountain, and then for you all the clocks and calendars will have finished their counting. Together with all my children, you will be mine and I will be yours forever.

## So, Be Glad God Has Promised to Make You A Winner

Recently our four-year-old grandson, John, accompanied his Uncle Jim on a sightseeing trip to O'Hare Field. After walking around the airport for awhile, little John tugged at his uncle's hand, and looking up with all earnestness said, "Uncle Jim, I'm hungry. I'm really, really, really— *really* hungry!"

That little episode prompts me to ask, "Are you glad you are a Christian? Really, really, really, *really* glad? And are you grateful for God's gift of love and His promise to declare you a winner when you cross the finish line?"

I end this quest for victory over life's struggles with another literary collectable. The author is unknown, but it's the best definition of Christianity I have ever found. If you are a believer, let its words sink deep into your spirit and give new vigor to your faith. If you have doubts, yet are wondering whether there just might be something to Christianity after all, don't hold back any longer. Ask God, as you read, to forgive your doubts and help you take that "leap of faith" that all believers take when they decide to follow Christ. Go back to that quiet place I suggested earlier, read this poem, and tell God you're ready. It will be the best decision of your whole life!

Christianity is not the religion of sorrow and gloom; it is the religion of the morning, and in its heart the happiness of Heaven.

Christianity is not a restraint but an inspiration; not a weight, but wings; not a subtraction but an addition.

Christianity brings bloom for faded hearts, rejuvenation for the prematurely old, imagination for the dry literal mind.

Christianity is not a kill-joy at the feast of life, not a kind of incarnate "don't." It bristles with great affirmatives, and fires the soul with permanent enthusiasms and durable loyalties.

Christianity leaves a trail of light wherever it goes; it can keep you cool under any confusion, bring you up smiling from any depth, and utterly banish your fret and worry.

Christianity brings zest and sparkle to life; it is sunshine on the flowers rather than darkness on the night; it is life abundant; it is leaving the little narrow life behind and leaving it forever!

—Unknown

At this point if someone were to ask you if you're glad you're a Christian, I trust your answer would be an enthusiastic, "Yes! I really, *really am!*"

So rejoice and know that no matter what happens between now and Heaven, you can count on God's promise that some day He will welcome you Home with open arms and declare you a winner!

# Credits

**Lloyd J. Ogilvie:** Be a First Stepper!
From *Congratulations: God Believes in You,* Dr. Lloyd Ogilvie,
© 1980, Word, Inc., Dallas, Texas. Used by permission.

**Catherine Marshall LeSourd:** Let God Take Charge
From *Beyond Our Selves;* © 1961 by Catherine Marshall.
Published by Chosen Books, Lincoln, VA 22078. Used by
permission.

**Joni Eareckson Tada:** My Wheelchair is My Classroom
Permission to reprint this article is granted by *Power for
Living,* © 1992 by Scripture Press Publications, Wheaton,
Illinois.

**Colleen Townsend Evans:** I Can't Get Along Without You,
Lord
From *A Deeper Joy,* by Colleen Townsend Evans, © 1982
by Colleen Townsend Evans. Published by Fleming H.
Revell Company, a Division of Baker Book House. Used
by permission.

**Paul Nowell Elbin:** Take Hold of Life and Live Every Minute!
From *Making Happiness a Habit.* © 1975 by Paul Nowell
Elbin. Excerpted by permission of the publisher, Abington
Press.

**Peter Kreeft:** The One Thing We Can't Live Without
From *The God Who Loves You.* © 1988 by Peter Kreeft. First
published as *Knowing the Truth of God's Love.* Published by
Servant Publications, Box 8617, Ann Arbor, Michi-
gan 48107. Used by permission.

**Henry Drummond:** The Greatest Thing in the World
From a condensed version of "The Greatest Thing in the World," by Henry Drummond, as published by Revell in *The Treasury of Inspirational Classics*, Bliss Albright, © 1923. Used by permission of Baker Book House.

**Ann Kiemel Anderson:** You Just Can't Stop Love!
Reprinted from *I'm Out to Change My World*, Ann Kiemel, © 1974 by Impact Books, a Division of John T. Benson Company, re-assigned to The Zondervan Corporation, 1982. Used by permission.


In addition to the above list, credit is given to The Chicago Sunday Evening Club, a television program broadcast on Channel 11, WTTW, Chicago—a program on which each of the following authors and pastors appeared in person on different dates to present his or her message, which later at my request, became one of the chapters in this anthology. Permission has been granted by both The Sunday Evening Club and the following authors and pastors: Nancy Becker, Joseph L. Bernardin, John R. Claypool, Everett L. Fullam, Richard C. Halverson, David S. Handley, Oswald C. J. Hoffmann, D. E. King, John Powell, and Woodie W. White. Credit is due also to Dorothy Cross, Harold Blake Walker, and Clyde O. York for their contributions.

Printed by Paraclete Press
Orleans, MA 02653
1-800-451-5006
FAX 508-255-5705